I0008191

Dating Diva Adventures

Dating Diva Adventures

I'm Not a Dating Expert. I've Just Dated More Than Most.

Lori Lemon-Geshay

Copyright 2010 Lori Lemon-Geshay

Paperback: 978-1-4583-9495-8

Hardback: 978-0-557-85583-4

While the author has made every effort to provide accurate telephone numbers and Internet addresses at the time of publication, neither party assumes any responsibility for errors, or for changes that occur after publication. Further, the publisher does not have any control over and does not assume any responsibility for third-party websites or their content.

HARRY WINSTON is a registered trademark of Harry Winston, Inc. This book is neither authorized by nor affiliated with Harry Winston, Inc.

Many of the designations used by manufacturers and sellers to distinguish their products are claimed as trademarks. Where those designations appear in this book and the publisher was aware of a trademark claim, the designations have been printed in capital letters.

For information about special discounts for bulk purchases, please contact lori_geshay@yahoo.com.

The Dating Diva can attend your live event. For more information or to book an event, contact NCB Productions and Public Relations at (713) 302-9828 or ncbrende@aol.com.

Dedication

May you choose to embrace the quest for true love and savor each breathtaking moment along the way.

Acknowledgments

Without knowing, you've played an integral role in the creation and journey of the Dating Diva. You've lavished me with unconditional love, trust, and incredible friendship. You chose to believe in my dream and became part of the adventure.

- To Nicole Brende for being a believer in true love.

- To Rasha Nasreddin for always believing in me.

- To Farnoush Forotan for being everything to me.

- To Diane Whorton-Brown for never ceasing to amaze and challenge me.

- To Kiana Tyler-Franks for listening to her heart and inspiring me as she lives out her own fairy tale.

- To Emily Seligmann, Missy Cayton, and Lana Herff for being my family and always loving me.

- To Stephen Allen, Nathan Bac, Michael Caplan, and Houston's own dynamo, Michael Chabala, for always providing such solid input and being incredibly loyal friends.

- To my father, although he's no longer with us, his spirit and endless love nourish my soul. For his love has motivated me to be fearless in my exploration of life and self-discovery.

With each of you, my life is full of love, adventure, and hope.

With each of you, the journey has been more exciting than I could've ever imagined.

What began as a mere dream is now my reality—*Dating Diva Adventures*!

Overview

A couple of years ago, I literally dreamt of *Dating Diva Adventures*! I awoke and quickly grabbed my orange Hermés journal next to my bed and sketched out the character image of the bathtub graphic that most associate the Dating Diva with today. After seven years of marriage and a recent end to a three-and-a-half-year relationship, I realized that I needed to rediscover who I was, what I wanted, and what I lacked in my life.

So I began writing about my many first dates, and the lessons learned along the way, on a well-known social networking site. What evolved? This book, *Dating Diva Adventures*, and a relationship advice column, "Ask the Dating Diva".

Introduction

I'm a girl who has everything that she wants, and nothing that she needs; that is, true love. I've had a successful IT sales career for over sixteen years and travelled around the world. However, I've paid too much attention to my job and not enough to my personal life. Why, you ask? I believed that money would bring me happiness. I believed that material things would make me whole, as I had grown up less than middle class in Georgia. I'm here to set the record straight that after all the extravagant purchases, you feel good for a moment, but then, not so much! Now don't get me wrong, I love my Birkins, diamonds, and anything with an interlocking "CC" (Chanel) symbol, but they don't keep me warm at night!

I began with three BFFs in tow, and we created an online dating profile for me with a well-known social networking site. After over 3,286 hits in thirty days, I set out on a journey of self-discovery in hopes to learn about human behavior, my needs, my desires, and basic human interaction. During this process of first dates, I met some incredible individuals and learned about common dating faux pas and areas of opportunity that we all have.

The book, *Dating Diva Adventures*, and my relationship advice column, "Ask the Dating Diva," are meant to be lighthearted, fun, and introspective. It is not about the "hunt for a man," nor is it about marriage or finding a rich sugar daddy. We'll leave that to the experts! I am a woman of substance, have my own financial means, and don't need a man for that, nor do you!

I am a simple girl who has lived a thousand lifetimes in friendship, love, and laughter, and can only hope that you'll enjoy my journey as it chronicles my quest for true love.

As I always say, I'm not a dating expert; I've just dated more than most!
XOXO

Contents

Let the Adventures Begin

L ike I said, I'm the girl who has everything she wants and nothing she needs—including the Birkin. Yes, it's divine, but it doesn't hug you back, believe it or not. Over two years ago, I decided to pursue love as I would everything else in my life—with adventure in my heart, zest, and enthusiasm. I did what every self-respecting single girl does— online dating! In the first four weeks, I had 3,286 hits and more e-mails to respond to than you can imagine. It was like having a job! What should a girl do? Call her girlfriends, of course! I enlisted three of my BFFs to assist in weeding through these stellar prospects. (Friend number one tells you like it is, and, ladies, it hurts. Friend number two—the detective—knows everything about them before the date. Friend number three just wants me to have fun and enjoy the journey.)

Let's start with the basics. I wore the same dress on every first date, I met at the same coffee shop, and I asked the same questions. Then I met a man who inspired me to hop on a plane and head to Washington DC for that first date. Could this be the connection I've waited for, or would this in fact be full-blown insanity kicking in?

Prior to arriving and meeting the mystery man, we (my three friends and I) established code words so that if someone else answered my phone, tried to be me, or say that I had stepped into the other room, they'd know that I wasn't OK. Code words are simple: "baseball"— I'm fine and I've hit it out of the park. "Purple"—like, ugh, black eye, not good … you get my point!

While on the plane, I spoke to the person sitting next to me and told her my story. I also pointed out that if I ended up on the 6:00 PM news tomorrow, she should remember my name. After deplaning and heading toward baggage claim, I enlisted the services of a police officer, gave him my business card, and asked him to meet this man with me, as I am a safety-conscious girl and had a master plan in place. When I met the mystery man, I photographed (via cell phone, of course) his government ID, license plate, and driver's license, and forwarded everything to my Number Three.

I arrived in DC, master security plan in place, and texted the code word to friend number three. I'd obviously seen the mystery man and thought, *wow, he looks better than his picture! Six foot, two—tall! Thank you, God!* He had dark blond hair and blue eyes. He was well groomed and dressed like he meant business. And he was cute!

So, with my Louis Vuitton in hand, I wheeled my luggage to the rear of his pickup truck and watched it land in the center of the flatbed. Yes, ladies, it was a pickup truck. I'm a southern belle, so, do I roll with this? Well, I grew up and went to college in New York City, so, in extreme panic, I politely requested that Louis V. be moved to the front cabin as it might rain. Yeah, that's it, it might rain. We'll roll with that!

I truly could care less what someone drives, as long as I look cute getting in and out of it. Kidding! Well, kind of. As we drove the beginner model Toyota, circa 1996 and with one hundred thousand miles on it, I realized that this date just has to be good—the power of positive thinking. I say to myself, *forget the stupid truck, you shallow girl; he's a great guy. Take your time and don't judge too quickly.*

We settled in for the ride into DC, and I finally remembered why I'd flown east—his wit and charm were completely captivating. (But please, do not think I'd forgotten about Louis V. in the rear, being treated like a second-class citizen.)

Tyler, as we'll refer to the mystery man, was a security consultant for the U.S. government specializing in setting up U.S. embassy networks across the world. His travel adventures were what encouraged me to initially begin conversations with him—and, of course, his good looks! Tyler's photos and stories of his adventures were thrilling to me. Tyler was eloquent and passionate about his work, his travels, and his accomplishments. All along he had been spontaneous, quirky, making me laugh until I cry, and seeming to enjoy life to the fullest, unlike people that typically cross my path. I believed that by viewing photos of him from Egypt, France, Australia, Turkey, and Israel, and from our thirty to forty days of conversations and e-mails, that he'd be somewhat more worldly than most. Not necessarily.

Someone once said that things aren't always as they appear. Was this the simple truth in the case of Tyler and my Washington DC adventure?

He was tall, muscular, handsome, and made me laugh like crazy! What had I missed? My intuition was telling me that something was off. I just couldn't pinpoint it.

In the midst of rush hour traffic, exhausted from a full day of work in Atlanta, and not to mention the delayed flight into DC, we decided to grab dinner earlier versus later. Tyler mentioned a quaint restaurant where we could dine outside and overlook the Potomac. This sounded perfect! We parked the truck and began to walk along a wooden walkway that led to the restaurant. The breeze, the sunset, and the roar of the planes kept us company as we arrived at the restaurant. Or should I say outdoor snack bar? Picnic-style tables, red plastic baskets of fried food, french fries, cold beer, and beef. What could be more appropriate on a first date, right? Was this happening? You've got to be kidding me! Did I just waste frequent flyer miles and a twenty-five dollar Charming Charlie's dress on this? (No laughing, ladies! As my dear friend, Leslie once told me, "It's not about the designer label on the dress, it's about the doll in the dress.") Oh well, simply a Southern girl, I rolled with it. I ordered every diet-lover's favorite—fried shrimp and french fries, along with my personal beverage staple, an ice-cold Amstel Light. Tyler ordered his meal and it was literally beef—just beef. Hum? No side of fries, baked potato, or veggies. Just beef! I couldn't help but ask, why? Tyler told me that he didn't eat anything but meat—ever. If you're in Texas, this could be a good thing, I guess. For me, it seemed a little strange. The more I began to query him about his eating habits, the more I realized that this was one quirky individual. Tyler told me that he didn't drink wine or coffee, and that he didn't eat dessert. What? A girl's gotta have her decadent chocolate fix, right? For Tyler, it was all about the meat. At least he was enjoying a beer, though. OK, everyone has quirks or interesting habits, but there's one thing that I've learned in my dating adventures, and that's good hygiene is mandatory!

Here's the thing, as Tyler and I talked, I noticed something—his teeth. I'm not referring to the front teeth, or the ones that are immediately visible, I'm referring to the interior teeth that you can only see when you're talking to someone. As my internal monologue kicked in, I was reminded of a song that I heard in preschool. "They call him yuck mouth, because he doesn't brush, how 'bout a little kiss?" I closed my eyes tightly, as if to turn off this inner monologue and focus on the conversation, but more importantly so that I couldn't see all the cavities and decay. How could I have missed this? Dear

Lord, get me out of here! Look, I was trying to be positive and keep an open mind, but good hygiene is just not an option.

I politely thanked Tyler for dinner as we walked back to the truck. I was confirmed on the last flight to New York at 11:00 PM, and he was generous enough to drive me back to the airport. As I said good-bye to Tyler, I very strategically dodged a good night kiss. I waved good-bye with my chin in the air and a smile on my face. Why, you ask? Because this is how this Southern girl rolls—with her Louis V. in tow! For every date, there are endless possibilities. In my case, there's New York City and a baseball player! Game on!

Kiss a Lot of Frogs

If a man e-mails, texts, or calls you to ask you for lunch, dinner, or for drinks, is that, in fact, a date? Or does he merely want to be friends because you understand him?

Well, funny thing—a man that I met recently through friends did all of the above and doesn't seem to think it counts as a date. I, for one, would like to know what his wife thinks. Yes, I said wife!

Why is it that men feel the need to make us all a tad bit skeptical? I have no answer to this question. Nor do I truly believe that any sane person would. Let's just leave it to good, old fashioned insecurity and stupidity on his part. Agreed?

I know that God has a better plan for me and that I must kiss a lot of frogs before I find my Prince Charming.

Gosh, I really hate warts!

The Bait Guy

Ladies, have you ever met a man and thought to yourself, *Wow, he's great but he's just not the one for me*? Maybe he's been coming on strong or he's not respecting your space—too much, too soon kind of thing?

We've all been there. You try and do the right thing by letting him know in a graceful and compassionate way, because you know what it feels like when he's just not that into you. Some guys just don't seem to get the hint. You explain that you're busy, your life is complicated, you've met someone else, but nothing seems to work. So then you decide that possibly the brutal truth might be the dose of reality that this guy needs. Ladies, in this instance, friendship is out of the question as this is a guy who won't get the hint. He consistently text messages, e-mails, and calls you, giving you reasons as to why you need to see him. Ladies, allow me to introduce you to the bait guy.

The bait guy will use any excuse to see you or speak to you. The bait guy can make you a star, get you a modeling gig, as he knows all the right people, connect you with the right people to help you put a business deal together, help get you a book deal, make you a reality TV star, and can introduce you to movie stars.

The bait guy has only his best interests at heart. He uses tactics that a five-year-old uses when playing with another child by taunting him with a toy. The bait guy is merely dangling your innermost desires in front of you. It's rather humorous if you really think about it. Like you're not going to figure it out. Desperation? Insecurity? Desire to conquer? I'm not quite sure I even care to define it.

Now don't get me wrong, if there's someone who truly can assist you in making your dreams come true, then good for you! Just make sure you're with this person for the right reasons.

Just remember that nothing is free, and unfortunately the bait guy does exist. So, my advice is, don't take the bait, take the fishing pole. You've already got the bait!

To Text or Not to Text

Suddenly, I started receiving e-mails from men regarding the need for dating advice—the dos and don'ts of dating. I'm no expert, but I do know a little about dating! Thirty-three first dates in the last one and a half years while doing research for my book might give me some credibility.

I received an e-mail from a married man who was debating with his single friends about what is the protocol for asking a girl out on a first date? To text, not to text, to e-mail, or to pick up the phone.

I'll keep this simple, guys—we don't care! It's not about the technology used, as we all abuse it profusely. It's about the action behind it. Tell us where you'd like to take us and tell us what time you'll be picking us up. Your actions speak volumes about the way that we'll be treated in the future. That is, if you don't take charge now, what does that mean for us in the future? Women want a man to be a man. Truly, we want you to! At times, you can tell us what you'd like us to wear to dinner or order our meal for us as a surprise. Believe it or not, that makes us feel even sexier than we already feel.

Again, don't overthink this! Isn't that what women tend to do?

Gentlemen, whether it's an e-mail, text message, or a smoke signal, just ask us out!

Love at First Sight

Within the last few days, I've been asked repeatedly if I believe in love at first sight.

As a hopeless romantic, I remember vividly the moment I met Thom. I had just started a waitressing job in Augusta, Georgia, around Masters week, and as it turned out, it was his first week on the job as well. I was bouncing around in my white cheerleading skirt and aqua polo shirt, then, suddenly I ran into him with my cocktail tray and nearly knocked him to the floor. When our eyes met, I remember this overwhelming feeling of sheer happiness, butterflies, and adrenaline! Trust me, this feeling was better than diamonds, new Choos, or that coveted Birkin bag—seriously! I don't think I've ever smiled quite like that before, either.

Later that evening when I saw my mother, I told her that I had just met the man I was going to marry. She laughed at me and then just walked away. Three months later, we were engaged and soon after married. I was fortunate to marry my very best friend and someone who I truly admired, but after seven years, we divorced. So now when people ask me if I believe in love at first sight, I say, yes, but it's the second, third, and fourth time that I have a problem with!

Clutch, Tote, or Hobo

In my quest for true love, there's a period of reflection that I have always welcomed. In recent months, I've had a ghost from dates past reappear via the almighty Facebook!

In this dating episode, we were casually introduced by friends who thought we'd hit it off. Well, we did! There was an immediate chemistry and a verbal banter that I long for to this very day. He was an intelligent, sexy man with amazing hair. He was charming and a very tangible human being. We dated for a while but eventually stopped seeing one another. I never knew why and made the decision never to ask, I guess because I wasn't in love with him. Although, he was hot!

After visiting his Facebook profile, I had a revelation, and finally I knew why we stopped seeing one another! The answer simply put— we had absolutely nothing in common! So I asked myself why I was not able to see it.

If anyone has viewed my Facebook profile, they'd think that I was merely a high-maintenance, Herve Leger–wearing little socialite who eats bonbons and works out at the Houstonian all day long. This is so not the case!

My point: appearances are only a small factor when dating. Don't get me wrong, chemistry and visual stimulation are important, though.

Ladies, it's kind of like shopping for a handbag—you're at Neiman Marcus, and suddenly you've spotted the perfect handbag! Your heart starts pounding, your eyes are glazed over, and you must have that handbag! The handbag is simply beautiful, made of the highest quality leather and embellished with semiprecious stones. It's heaven! You give the sales associate your card and depart the store with such pride, like you've climbed Mount Everest. Later that evening, while admiring your "investment," you realize that none of your things will fit in the bag—not your Blackberry, Hermés journal, makeup bag, Evian Brumisateur, nothing. Prior to purchasing this limited edition handbag, all you had to do was open it up and place some of your own items in the bag just to make sure it would hold all of your things. So ask yourself next time you're going on a date—are you a clutch, tote, or a hobo? As for me, I've discovered that I'm a Jimmy Choo watersnake tote. Happy shopping!

Late Night to Date Night

For those of you who have grown up in Houston and have ever hit the club scene, you'd know that Michael Caplan's Club Uropa has been a nightlife staple and our own little version of Cheers for over thirteen years. However, Club Uropa recently held their "End of an Era Party," which, by far, was one of the most unique events of the year. It was a mix of old, new, and *Tales from the Crypt*. It was a phenomenal evening spent with five hundred of my closest friends. The drinks were flowing, music pumping, and hands a-groping—they didn't call it Club 'You-Grope-A' for nothing, right?

As with any nightclub, there's always a little drama that ensues as 2:00 AM approaches. Frankly, it wouldn't be the same without it. Men start gravitating toward what's closest to the money, women grab their girlfriends then rush to the bathroom to freshen up and ask, *why is he acting that way? Why doesn't he see what a great girl I am?* Ladies, stop! You're wasting your breath. This is not the venue to meet your future husband. Their actions are not about you or what you may or may not lack. The men you'll meet in a nightclub are there to have a great time, drink with the boys, check out hot girls, and hopefully get lucky.

So the question is: where do you go to meet men who want more than a good time? Remember how hard you worked to accessorize that absolutely fabulous Dolce & Gabbana dress? You found the perfect Giuseppe Zanotti shoes, subtle, yet elegant jewelry, and spent hours at the spa getting your hair done, a manicure and pedicure, and the perfect spray tan. Acquiring the knowledge to shop for and create the ensemble didn't happen overnight, did it? No, it took years of trial by fashion faux pas, shopping at low-end to high-end stores from Forever 21 to Tootsies. Today you know who you are, what your signature silhouette is, and what your overall style is, right? Try shopping in venues that are representative of you. You're no longer the Forever 21 or Arden B. girl, so stop acting like it! If you're looking for that amazing Yves Saint Laurent dress, did you really think you were going to find it at Kmart? I didn't think so. Ladies, embrace your inner Bergdorf blonde, and as always, happy shopping!

The Love-Affair Stare

Recently, I was reminded of someone from my past who I had purposely tucked away in my memory for safekeeping. And wow, what a lovely memory!

Many years ago, I lived in New York City and worked for Elizabeth Arden-Red Door Salon. (Gratis services—what an incentive!) I had finished my shift and hopped the subway to head home. As with any subway ride, I typically keep my head down and am cautious not to make eye contact with anyone. On this day, that tiny tidbit of common sense went out the window. While seated comfortably, I glanced across the subway car to see what appeared to be an Adonis. I felt unusually drawn to this man. There was something about him that was familiar, and that prompted me to stare at him. My mystery man was six foot two, with a slender, yet elegant build, black hair, and he was Latin! He had the perfect tan, like he had just returned from St. Barts. As I studied his flawless face, I could see that I was making him uncomfortable. I was able to recognize that he was intrigued by my bold yet brazen attitude, and suddenly the game was on. He smiled and I countered with a coy yet flirtatious smirk. This was the most daring thing I had ever done. How liberating! The train ride continued on, as did my staring.

As the subway car arrived at the final stop, I rose from my seat to exit the subway car. He followed. To my surprise, he spoke! He introduced himself and we chatted for a while. He seemed incredibly charming, and seeing that he has missed his subway stop—about twenty minutes earlier—I was compelled to accept his invitation for coffee. We left the platform to head upstairs. We found a nearby coffee shop and sat for a couple of hours to talk. Without question, there was an enormous chemistry and intellectual dialogue that was beyond stimulating. As the night continued, we decided to depart the coffee shop and head to his favorite little Italian restaurant on the lower East Side. This restaurant was incredibly romantic and cozy. The mussels marinara and red snapper Veneziana were heavenly. The pinot noir was endless and so was the conversation. He was utterly fascinating. He was well-travelled, educated, and enrolled at NYU Law preparing to take the bar exam. I couldn't imagine a more perfect evening. However, this man surpassed all of my expectations! After dinner, we headed toward the foot of the Brooklyn Bridge and walked along the water. It was like a movie! We spent the entire night walking and talking, from Wall Street, Little Italy, Chinatown, SoHo, and all the way toward NYU. By this point it must have been 4:00 AM, so we stopped at his friend's dorm room and cleaned up. We headed out about an hour later and spent the early morning hours near the Intrepid, watching the sunrise. It was the most romantic date of my life.

Our story continued as we dated successfully for many months. We spent every possible moment together—plays, jazz clubs, museums, the library, running, softball, and touch football in Central Park. To this day, I'll never forget how he taught me how to navigate my way through Central Park by looking at the lampposts, or the simple pleasures of the carousel and duck pond.

As the bar exam approached, his ability to spend time with me became nonexistent but certainly understandable. The big day arrived and he was successful. On his first attempt, he passed the exam! I was so proud of him. The offers started pouring in and the world was at his feet—our feet. To celebrate the occasion, he invited me to South America on a two-week vacation. Due to my schedule with school and my many jobs, I was unable to accept the generous invitation. The day he left, I was thrilled that he was going with friends from school. This was an adventure of a lifetime for all of them. The day he returned—now that's another story.

Two weeks passed and we finally got to see one another. The reunion wasn't what you'd expect. He was distant but kind. He explained, "We need to talk; I've met someone on the trip." He planned to move in with her in Brooklyn Heights! Ugh, my heart was breaking! Did you hear it? Did you feel it too? I had enormous tears in my eyes and couldn't allow him to see them fall down my cheeks.

This was the love affair that every girl dreams of. The perfect first date. The perfect everything, including the perfect ending. I must recognize that we ended it the way it began, with sincerity, class, respect, and friendship. His last words to me were, "You are a beautiful work in progress and I can't wait to see you in five years, as I know you'll do great things." He was an amazing man; a man who was able to muster up the courage to tell me the truth, although a devastating truth.

Many years had passed and I was walking along Park Avenue South near Thirty-first Street, and to my surprise, he was walking toward me! My heart was pounding as he approached. We stopped to talk and I discovered that he's no longer practicing law. He opted to, in his words, "make a difference," and is now a sixth grade teacher at a nearby school. As always, his heart was open and his aptitude for compassion was stronger than before. He was no longer with the same woman, but I was soon-to-be engaged to my Giants football player. We said our good-byes, and as I turned to walk away, he told me that our paths will cross again.

Reader Comment from Facebook:

All the romance and glamour, do you realize just how many women only *dream* of this kind of life? Your Dating Diva is a great escape for these others out there who have only to dream. Keep on keepin' on, sunshine.

Cowboy Up, Houston

The quest for love continues and so does my belief that my knight in shining armor is out there. I'm determined that nothing will stand in my way. I have an open mind and an open heart. However, common sense remains intact.

I recently met someone through a friend. He seemed quite nice as we spoke through telephone calls and e-mail chats. In the spirit of full disclosure, I told him about my column. I didn't want him to be blindsided on our first date, right?

So, he had been reading the "Dating Diva Adventures" and providing a man's perspective. We agreed to finally meet for lunch. He was pleasant, decent-looking, and the conversation was easy. As the lunch continued, he told me how much he'd like to see me again. I said to myself, *What the heck, he seems like a nice enough guy*. After I accepted the invitation for the second date, he proceeded to tell me that he was currently in a relationship and wanted to be up front with me. He didn't want me to get the wrong idea, as he'd like to have me as a friend.

Wrong idea? Lunch with someone you met through a friend? Telephone conversations? E-mails? Second date invitation? How could I possibly get the wrong idea? I'm blonde, but the peroxide hasn't caused permanent brain damage yet. His ignorance was perplexing as was his arrogance.

Why are we always looking for the bigger, better deal? Why can't we be appreciative of what we have? Let me say this, when I find my Mr. Right, I'll most definitely recall these incidents and respect my partner, our relationship, and myself.

Is this my lesson in the quest for love? Respect? Or, is it to conduct a background check on every man before I go out with them? Should I require that they fill out a questionnaire prior to the date? You've got to fill out paperwork prior to entering your horse at the Houston Livestock Show and Rodeo, right? Why not before a date?

Wait! Maybe I've got it all wrong! It's not a knight in shining armor that I'm looking for, it's a cowboy! Cowboys are known to be honest, hardworking, loyal, appreciative, and know how to treat a lady with respect! Oh, it's time to buckle up. I might even need a pair of chaps after this one. Cowboy up, Houston. I'll see you at the rodeo!

The Scent of a Man

S ome men will say to learn the most about a woman all you need to do is spend about five minutes studying her vanity area. I believe this to be true.

No one can deny that women are mysterious creatures. We have lotions, creams, and fragrances that could hold their own with any Neiman Marcus cosmetics counter. Yes, that includes me!

Personally, my Waterford crystal vanity of fragrances has about fifteen bottles of perfume from Coco Chanel, Chanel #5, Michael by Michael Kors, Allure, and Clive Christian.

Earlier today, when spritzing my personal favorite, I was taken back in time and reminded of a signature scent long forgotten—the scent of a man!

There's a man who crossed my path many years ago. The stereotypical tall, dark, and handsome description. Truly, a lovely creature to admire. We dated for nearly a year, and the unfortunate thing is that we really had nothing in common. Meaning I wanted more and he wanted nothing! This man possessed the most natural sex appeal out of anyone I've ever encountered. His appeal was not defined by a full head of hair, chiseled features, or a body like Michael Phelps, it was his scent! Back then, if I were ever in a room and he appeared, I'd know it without even seeing his face. He was simply magnetic. To this day, no other man has ever had that effect on me. This makes me wonder: do men have the same sensual senses and recollections that women do? Are men truly attracted to a women's scent? Does it matter?

Reader Comments from Facebook:

Andrew from California: "I remember being in elementary school and meeting Tara at the playground. To this day, any time I smell the scent of Love's Baby Soft, it takes me back in time."

Jake from Texas: "Tammy's hair shined like that of an angel's and smelled like cotton candy. So, I married her!"

Patti from Georgia: "I used to love to wear my boyfriend, Michael's, Atlanta Braves T-shirt. It smelled like him and made me feel safe. The day I washed it, I cried."

What's Your Dating FICO Score?

Have you ever gone to a FedEx Office store and picked up your job order and then later in the day received a telephone call to make sure you were satisfied with your order?

Have you ever gone to the dentist and shortly after received a call following up on the visit?

Have you ever taken your car in for servicing and received a follow-up survey in the mail from a quality assurance representative?

So why is it that single men (or women) don't come with some sort of a quality assurance plan or satisfaction-based references?

You need solid experience and a well-written résumé when interviewing for your dream job. The initial interview is typically followed by a request for professional references, right? So why aren't we associating that same philosophy in our personal lives? I know, I know, there's Google, Dog Pile, and LinkedIn, but who wants to violate someone's personal privacy? I'm not Blue Moon Detective Agency, for goodness sake!

We have social networking sites such as eHarmony, Match, MySpace, and Facebook, yet nothing on hard-core personal and factual relationship data. I cannot seem to fathom why some IT guru hasn't created a relational database that tracks people, places, patterns, likes, dislikes, and most importantly, red flags! It's all about Business Intelligence (BI) in this economy. Why not make dating about Personal Intelligence (PI)? You don't buy a car without researching the cars in the same class, right? You research it! Let's have this same approach when dating. This venture is unbelievably complex and farfetched, I realize. In a perfect world this would be the personal résumé of your life. Do you think Equifax and TransUnion would be interested?

Now ask yourself, what would your dating FICO score be?

Dating in Your Age Bracket

As a Houston transplant and someone who has lived in thirteen different states with numerous jobs and job titles, it would take a very well-rounded individual to peak my interest. I'm a girl who can throw on a baseball cap, T-shirt, and jeans with my Chucks or slip on a cocktail dress and feel simply spectacular in either. I'm what one might refer to as a chameleon. New York City, Chicago, Miami, Los Angeles, or the backwoods of Georgia, I've done it all. I have many different interests, my own opinions, and enjoy the art of intelligent, meaningful conversation. Each of these is a part of what makes me unique, creative, independent, and perfect in my imperfections.

The challenge is that I need someone who's willing to get to know all of me, along with my numerous imperfections!

After going on thirty-three first dates in the last year and a half, I've learned something that I refer to as dating within your age bracket. It's basically a review of your personality, likes, and dislikes, followed by a quick reference guide so that you can cut to the chase!

So my advice is to refer to the quick reference guide, but take it with a grain of salt. Remember, we are all accountable for our dates, as we accepted the invitation!

Dating In Your Age Bracket: Quick Reference Guide

Men 25–30 Years of Age:

You'll enjoy two-dollar beer, Mexican food, karaoke, and college football at local sports bars. (Hook 'em, Horns!)

Men 30–35 Years of Age:

You'll enjoy sushi, bars, dance clubs, boating, and "you're the boat, babe," along with three other gorgeous girls. Basically, you're arm candy! Look at it like a music video shoot without the fifty-dollar daily rate. Now you might need to bring your own credit card as you sometimes go dutch. Too bad you didn't get the daily rate!

Men 35–40 Years of Age:

Dating? They don't do dating or relationships! It's about hanging out. In most cases, you'll need to reference age brackets twenty-five through thirty-five. Motto: get your own meal and I'll see you after the clubs. Text message you at 2:00 AM, "U out?"

Men 41–55 Years of Age:

Most men in this age bracket know how to wine, dine, and make you feel spectacular; like you're the only woman in the world. They are not afraid of a real woman. Ladies, you don't need to dumb yourself down in this age bracket. These men treat a lady like a lady. They've not forgotten how to open a door or politely pull out your chair for you when you dine. They have the game down to a science. Some are still noncommittal and afraid of their own shadow. They say everything you want/need to hear in order to seal the deal! Caution: there's no long-term contract here, and no residual commissions are paid. Read the fine print, research historical data, and understand its relevance.

Men 56 and Above:

AARP is mentioned at least once in conversation, as is the nursing home that they've been touring for a "relative." They need to find a mate—and soon—as they won't be able to carry their own oxygen tank in the coming years!

DDA Disclaimer:

No scientific study has been performed. This is not approved for individuals without a sense of humor. To protect the innocent, all names and personal references have been removed. If you think this is about you, it's not, so don't ask. Just reinvent your age bracket!

Great Love

As I continue to write about my quest for true love, I now understand that until I share this story with you, you can never fully understand why I'm so certain that not only does true love exist, but most importantly, *great love* exists! This supernova of an adventure was romantic, complex, and an overwhelmingly emotional period in my life. No one knows, as this story has never been told.

As a girl who grew up in the backwoods of Georgia, I always knew that I was not only supposed to travel to France, but that something extraordinary would happen there. It's as though something inside me ached for the city. For years, I had purchased books on Paris and started creating a list of where I wanted to go, what I'd hoped to see, and the museums that I must tour. Understand that where I grew up and attended school, we didn't have art appreciation classes. To dream of anything other than marrying your high school sweetheart was like expecting to win the lottery. It was a point in my life where I was once again on my own. I was no longer married and was financially able to make my dream into a reality. So on a whim, I jetted off to Paris for a couple of weeks in search of *me*.

It was a summer afternoon like no other. I was sitting at an outdoor cafe near Rue Dauphine. There was a man sitting about two tables away. He was incredibly focused on what appeared to be a journal of some sort. He was writing feverishly until suddenly he looked over and caught my gaze. Once he saw me, I abruptly looked away and attempted to look busy by preparing my coffee. Moments later, the waiter appeared with a single red rose. The waiter explained that it was from a man at a nearby table. As I inquired about which table, the man—that man—appeared in front of me. He introduced himself as Jean Paul and without invitation joined my party of one.

Jean Paul was a writer and a painter. He was 6'1" tall, with jet-black, wavy hair and alluring, green eyes and a small scar above his left eyebrow. He was dressed quite casually in a fitted gray T-shirt, jeans, and a lightweight scarf with black shoes. His accent was distracting because he could literally undress me with the mere sound of his voice. He was sophisticated but not in a regal way. It was more of a life experience- type of sophistication; one that is learned.

Jean Paul and I sat at the cafe talking for hours. Although his accent was hypnotic, I was able to focus and learn of his recent travels to New York City, where he was fortunate enough to land a small showing at a gallery in SoHo. He had been writing a book about his travels and shared stories of his most exciting memories. Jean Paul had grown up just outside the city of Paris. He had hoped to move to New York to promote his work in the next year or so. As twilight grew near, he told me of a nearby gallery where he had some work displayed. Without hesitation, I agreed to accompany him. I think we must have walked for about thirty minutes or so. As we approached the gallery, the one thing that caught my eye was the architecture of the building. It looked almost like a smaller scale home, and the buildings adjacent to it were apparently added in much later years. The character of the building was warm, intriguing, and full of history. As we entered, I was able to identify which pieces were his based on his visual examples from earlier in the day. The color, texture, light, and somber feeling were representative of where he was in his life when he painted these pieces. They were unusually moving, especially if you knew the stories behind the work.

For the days and weeks to come, we were inseparable. He was a calming force, intelligent, generous in nature, and incredibly expressive. Not to mention that he was a fantastic tour guide with a motorcycle. Paris, a sexy, artistic man, and a motorcycle—now this was like a movie!

The city was electric and completely intoxicating. It is the most romantic city in the world, and he made it ever so magical. Jean Paul and I toured the Louvre, visited the Opera Garnier, and dined at Le Procope. (While at Le Procope, we invited another couple to join us as they were eager to practice speaking English.) We packed a picnic lunch, sat on the steps of Notre Dame, strolled the Champs Elysees, and even played in the fountains to cool off, as many Europeans do. We walked along La Conciergerie holding hands, visited the Sacre Coeur, and of course, visited the Tour Eiffel. I remember sitting underneath the Tour Eiffel admiring the bright lights. We sat, laughing at the day's events, in which we were nearly kicked out of a prestigious gallery. Don't ask why! It was a tourist's dream, but my reality.

It was my final evening in Paris. As we approached the Seine, there was a beautiful boat that was waiting there. All along, I'd thought that we were merely going to walk along the Seine. I couldn't believe Jean Paul had everything planned to the last detail. At that time, it was the most romantic night of my life and one that shall remain personal and private. To speak of it would somewhat tarnish or devalue it.

My time in Paris had come to an end. I knew that saying good-bye to Jean Paul wasn't going to be an easy task. From the first moment, I told myself not to get too close. This was a two-week adventure compared to a lifetime of heartache. Romance like this isn't reality. The problem was that my head wasn't communicating with my heart. As I kissed Jean Paul good-bye and stepped into the taxi, he promised that we'd see one another soon. He told me that he loved me and regretfully should've told me sooner. As the taxi door closed, I could feel this sense of sorrow come over me. I waved good-bye and the taxi pulled away.

After returning home, I received several calls and letters from Jean Paul. He wanted me to return to Paris. If not, he was coming to the United States. Although I desperately wanted to see him again, I thought it best to let Paris remain in Paris. This was a fairy tale. It was emotionally draining. I truly didn't think that he was serious. I thought it was a summer fling. I believed that things would cool down and the calls would inevitably become fewer. I'm not quite sure when or why, but my heart took over and I finally returned his call. At that moment, I allowed myself to love and recognize that this was the real deal. Then the unexpected happened—the phone rang and Jean Paul's mother answered. She knew immediately who I was and said that she had hoped I would call. I could tell that she was sad but couldn't comprehend why, as I was overly excited to speak with Jean Paul. Within what seemed like a fraction of a second, my world crumbled as she told me that Jean Paul had been killed in a motorcycle accident the day before. As I fell to the floor in utter shock, she said that he had every intention of coming to the United States, and in his own words, had said that I was his great love.

As I mentioned when I began this story, it's one that I have never spoken of, out of shame, shock, disbelief, who knows? It was too unbelievable to believe. The only thing I am confident of is that this is how I know that great love exists. It knows no boundaries or borders. It calls you and you must respond to it. I selfishly turned my back on it once and let it slip away. I understand that we have today and that tomorrow may not exist. I had the incredible fortune to be captivated by great love, if only briefly. Jean Paul seems like a lifetime ago, and it wasn't until the last one-and-a-half years that I revisited that period in my life and began my "Quest." By doing so, I was able to discover a far greater appreciation for his last words to me—"Regretfully, I should have." Seek, respect, cherish, and never regret. Great love does exist!

READER COMMENT FROM FACEBOOK:

Loved it even though it made me cry!

Great story. Thanks for your courage in sharing it with us.

Truly speechless, a great love is hard to find. This is written with such a refreshingly vulnerable tone, and so eloquent. An amazing story, I wish you all the best in finding such passion and joy with love and life in your future!

A Cowboy and a Gentleman

For those of you keeping up with my recent Dating Diva Adventures, you'd know that I've been spending a lot of time at the Houston Livestock Show and Rodeo. I've realized that certain things I hold in high regard when it comes to dating are here! Yes, truly, in our great state of Texas—passion, determination, integrity, and chivalry. Unknowingly, the words define a cowboy and a gentleman!

Ladies, if you've never watched a cowboy ride a bull, you don't know what you're missing. These men are incredibly passionate and determined. These men wake up every morning to say, "I think I'll risk my life today and ride a bull." They know that they could potentially break their neck, or succumb to something far worse. I find their zest for life and extraordinary focus to be very appealing qualities. It's sexy, right?

I wonder, is being a cowboy a state of mind or is it an affair of the heart? Look at the three- and four-year-old Mutton Busters. These tiny tots, all dressed in cowboy gear, wrap their limbs around a sheep and they hold on for dear life. Ten seconds later, they're on the underbelly of the sheep, and then suddenly, flat faced in red dirt. Are these our future cowboys and bull riders? I sure hope so, because the pure spirit they exude is that of a real cowboy. Let us applaud our 2010 Mutton Busters!

The cowboys I've encountered in recent weeks don't have designer dirt on their boots from some real estate development that they've just toured. Their jeans aren't Lucky Brand, and their Stetsons weren't purchased at Cavendar's two hours before the barbecue cook-off, unlike mine! These cowboys have been taking care of cattle all day and farming the land. They understand hard work and respect and have appreciation for where they hang their hat. Seriously, how many people do you know who could give you a history lesson of the state in which they reside? Ask a cowboy, I bet he could! Cowboys, at least the ones I've encountered, have been nothing but chivalrous. They pick me up on our dates; they open my door for me, and pull out my chair. Aren't these all the things mothers teach their sons when they first start dating? What has happened to these beautiful little reminders that reaffirm we're special to the person we're dating? These simple acts of kindness and chivalry make it known that they'll care for us and protect us. Let me add, I like being treated like a lady. In fact, I demand it! If you want my attention, act like a man, or rather, a gentleman!

As I've said, spending time at the Houston Livestock Show and Rodeo has been somewhat of an epiphany. As a reformed country girl who moved to the big city at the age of eighteen in search of education, life experience, great love, and success, I am suddenly realizing that the things I value most have been in front of me all along. I just didn't recognize them. Stubborn pride mixed with a dose of pure stupidity, I guess.

This experience has allowed me to take a step back in time. It's my first date and I'm so excited! Do you remember that feeling? I don't know about you, but I was jumping out of my skin. I couldn't wait to take his hand and step up into that fire engine-red pickup truck. I knew I'd be spending time with someone who valued me and would care for me. That was a genuine and precious feeling. Even today, as I listen to country music (Brad Paisley, Keith Urban, and Darrius Rucker), I get swept away with the naïve notion that the lyrics could be a reality. Again, it's that hopeless romantic in me and probably why my father always said I'd end up being a country-western singer one day. (Not to mention that I was Mississippi state champion three years in a row!) Being around country music, cowboys, and the rodeo has nurtured my soul.

I think when we're younger, we look to explore the world, reinvent ourselves, and figure out who we are. What if who we really are has been inside us all along, yet we're just too arrogant to recognize it? What if my journey has led me to Texas to find that unique mix of city, cowboy, and hot-blooded Texan?

I'm thankful for recent recollections, and thus have a far greater appreciation for our great state of Texas, but most importantly, growing up in the South with good values, great music, and good men!

Now understand, I'll always be the girl who wears Jimmy Choo snakeskin stilettos and Herve Leger. However, nothing feels better than putting on my twenty-one-year-old Justin boots and drinking a cold beer. Guess you really can't take the country out of the girl; you just merely wipe off the red dirt and add some highlights!

Here's to continuing my quest for love and maybe even roping my own cowboy and a gentlemen!

Watch out, boys, I just bought a lasso—from Neiman's, of course!

Aloha

In my quest for love, something fairly amazing happened. I refer to it as "Aloha."

Last year marked a very significant birthday and a time in my life when I longed to be close to my father. Although he is no longer with us, there are still times when I need to feel closer to him and to the life that he once led. When this happens, I book a flight to California. This is my time to reflect and to find a sense of peace that I can only seem to find while at the beach. The ocean seems a lot like life to me—especially dating. Some men, like waves, roll in and out of your life unexpectedly.

While on this journey, I had the good fortune to meet up with a man who I had worked closely with for many years. He had heard of my visit and its relevance and had suggested that we meet up.

Now, in a professional setting, I'm not one to let my guard down: business is business. However, this was no longer business as I was resigning from our company in three days, so meeting up was no big deal—or was it?

It was another spectacular California day. I'd already kicked it off with a brisk walk and a chai tea latte. My cell phone rang, and it was him. He said that, he was just up the beach. So I doubled back and saw him walking toward me. At first glance, he was a hot mess! He was fumbling with his keys, coffee, wallet, and cell phone. It seemed odd as he had always been a man "in control." His behavior made me laugh and allowed for a rather enthusiastic greeting.

As we walked along the beach, the conversation was completely off topic, meaning off work topic. I felt completely comfortable and, frankly, not like my usual self. Maybe it was the beach, the breeze, or the romantic notion of it all, but I was having a great time. I had never allowed myself to look at this man in a romantic fashion before, but suddenly I was. Could I alter my vantage point now? What was I thinking? I know him and his history. He was like a pair of leopard-print Christian Louboutin boots that are elusive, wild, utterly sexy, yet *not* for everyday wear! Funny thing, you're still curious about the boots! You have to try them on to see if they fit, right? Are they comfortable? Can you afford to live without them?

This was an ubersexy man with a plan! He told me that he wanted to take me kayaking. I was thrilled as I had hoped to spend as much time outdoors as possible. (Note: I'm the quintessential indoor girl who has suddenly become an outdoor girl.) So the date continued, and we got geared up, grabbed the kayak, and hit the water. I sat in the front of the kayak and did my very best to push forward, while he was in the back with a much better view. Not fair! The conversation continued, and the stories surrounding our exes began. They quickly defined "who we were" and "who we are now." For someone who had appeared to be so complex, he was suddenly transparent.

As my arms began to tire, he took control and led us toward something incredibly simple to most but simply fantastic to me—the seals! As I mentioned before, I wanted to feel closer to my father. What he didn't know is that my father had always taken me to see the seals when I was a little girl. With this gesture, he had unknowingly made my trip and our visit even that much more special. As we sat in the kayak and talked for a bit, I sensed that my walls were coming down. I was relaxed, maybe a little goofy, and blissfully happy, and in such a simple setting. Wait, I can be happy outside of Neiman Marcus! Is this possible?

By the time we returned, we were wet, hungry, and ready to head back toward Laguna Beach. I was desperate to get the sand off me, so I invited him back to freshen up. Afterward, we decided to walk around Laguna. We ended up at a little sushi restaurant where we grabbed a light bite, a few beers, and just hung out for a while. Then the unexpected happened: he opened up to me. He felt the need to tell me about himself. He disclosed some very personal details and things that he believed might prompt me *not* to see him again.

He said that he didn't want me to hear it from anyone else. It was almost like a warning: "As-Is, No Warranty." I explained to him that everyone travels his own path. The lessons we learn make us who we are today. If it weren't for everything that he had been through, whether good or bad, he wouldn't be who is today. Trust me; I'm the last person to judge anyone. (Remember, thirty-three first dates for this book!) Frankly, I was amazed that this man felt the need to take off his mask and show me his true self. I appreciated him even more. What he wasn't aware of is that I already knew this information, yet it didn't matter to me.

To my surprise, the date wasn't over yet. He wanted to take me to dinner. I didn't have any other plans, so I accepted. We headed back to the room. I freshened up and allowed him to do the same. At dinner, to my surprise, he had remembered that my birthday was earlier in the week. A birthday cake appeared at the table, and the festivities began—or shall I say the embarrassment? Was this guy for real? How could I have overlooked such a caring and easygoing guy? Dinner was over, but the night had just begun.

We headed toward the beach and sat along the wall, watching the stars and listening to the waves. The night could not have been more perfect, until he kissed me. On a scale from 1–10, it was off the charts! Wow, his lips were strong, full, and warm. So sexxy! (Yes, he deserved a double x.) The chemistry was fantastic, as was the emotion behind the kiss. He was ever so sincere and could've caused me to faint if he had continued! This was by far the most unexpected and exciting date in a long time. It made all the bad "adventure dates" worthwhile.

The next day arrived and life was as it was. Reality is ever so cruel, right? I began to analyze the date. Isn't that what women do? What do I do now? Where can this go? I live in Texas. What am I thinking?

The days went by, as did the weeks, and then months. Our ability to keep up the pace was less than stellar. We extended an occasional call, text, or voicemail message. Then one day, it all became clear to me: like the oceans waves, this man couldn't stay. I like to call him "Aloha." Aloha is a man that you don't know whether to say hello or good-bye to. He is the essence of the wave. He rolls into your life and, after a breathtaking moment, rolls out again. It's beautiful while it lasts, As is, Aloha!

Fairy-Tale Beginnings

Love stories aren't always the ones you read about or the ones depicted in a Nora Roberts's Lifetime movie event. Sometimes love stories are the ones that we live day-to-day; however, we're so distracted by the minutiae, we fail to recognize and appreciate what's already in our grasp.

Thanks to various Disney movies, we've been led to believe that a fairy-tale prince will rescue us from a dragon or give us a perfect kiss that will awaken us from an evil witch's spell. Even as adults, we believe that candles, flowers, romantic music, and tokens of one's affection are gestures of real love. Although appreciated, I'm here to dispute this myth. Love comes in many forms (some mentioned above); the rarest is that of respect, compassion, compromise, and one's actions in times of need.

While on my own personal quest for love, I was able to let a dear friend look through my crystal ball and see that she was living the greatest·love story of all—her own. This story isn't consumed with romantic overtures: it's filled with the reality of everyday life.

When dating, we consistently work to makeover our partner. We look to change them, whether it is their personal style, grooming habits, leaving the toilet seat up, or learning to become more considerate of one another.

My dear friend had been dating a man for over eight years. They lived together, on and off, because she constantly moved in and moved out. Like most women, she was in and out due to one of the following reasons: (1) he didn't put gas in the car when he drove it, (2) he cooked dinner for *himself*, (3) he made *himself* a cup of coffee, (4) he didn't show enough affection or emotion, or (5) he was not romantic enough. Personally, I believe that all of these things *are* important, but at what cost? Where is the compromise? What do you value most?

My dear friend truly loved this man. She had been in the dark as to his daily activities because of the nature of his job. She had never been able to say, "Honey, tell me about your day." She'd had to find other topics of conversation and areas of interest. For eight years, she had loved this man and believed that he was her one true love. I had been by her side, understood her frustrations, and empathized with her. These were things that she needed that she wasn't getting out of the relationship.

After eight years together, the relationship ended, and she immediately thrust herself into another. On the outside looking in, it seemed like a fairy tale come to life. The new man lavished her with extravagant gifts like cars, diamonds, and a work-free lifestyle. He quickly asked her to marry him and life seemed perfect. The new relationship rapidly turned toxic—like a poisoned apple. This new man was the polar opposite to the previous. The new man had a very controlling and overbearing *Sleeping with the Enemy* style. When the two decided to have a child, she was forced to deal with some health issues that, until then, had been unknown to her. When the fiancé learned of these issues, he immediately cast her aside, like damaged goods. She was left to feel that her value was no longer significant.

With any substantial relationship, friendship should always remain intact. In my opinion, it shows one's true character, meaning the manner in which you enter the relationship should be the manner in which you exit the relationship. My dear friend shared this graceful quality and so did her ex of eight years. So when in need, she called her ex and was welcomed back into his life. This incredible man who had previously had a fear of commitment and an inability to put anyone before himself was suddenly called to task. This man had the magnificent fortitude to be *the* man that every girl dreams of. This man stepped back into her life, without skipping a beat, and took care of her. He was forced to make life-altering decisions on her behalf. A man who probably never thought he had the capacity to nurture was able to rise to the occasion when it mattered and be the most courageous of men. One might even say a fairy tale's Prince Charming.

While having lunch with my dear friend, she once again told me how she loved this man, how he was always there for her, and how the dynamics of the relationship had changed. Yet in the next breath, she began nitpicking those aforementioned things. She discussed moving out and into a beautiful high-rise condominium.

In that very instant, it hit me. I explained to her that for eight years she had been in and out of the relationship. This man, in a time of utmost need, had been there for her. Even after everything, he still wanted to be with her and start a family. Yet, she was sitting in front of me wanting to move out. I asked her how she could ever expect this man to give her what she needs, if she can't give him what he needs. If she was always leaving, why would he ever let his guard down, allow her to captivate his heart, or put her first when he feared rejection or exposing himself to the possibility of abandonment? When you're constantly running away from the one thing that you want, how can you be expected to catch it—or for it to catch you?

For years, this lovely couple has had a push-and-pull-type relationship. No matter what, they've fought their way back to one another in the most difficult of circumstances. They've stood by one another in times of great need and sorrow. They've learned to stop running and start laughing. They've learned that tiny imperfections are what make us all unique and interesting. They've learned compassion, compromise, and that they can put one another first. They've learned to depend on each other and relinquish total control. This lovely couple has experienced what most married couples never have to go through.

I know that they will have a strong marriage because it'll be based on reality and not a Disney fairy tale. It'll be based on friendship, respect, communication, compromise, compassion, and genuine love.

My dear friend has decided that the minutiae will no longer get in her way. She realized that everything she's been fighting for is within her grasp. She's realized that she can never live her own fairy tale if she's always running away and focusing on things that don't matter. She's decided to let her man be the man that he's proven himself to be. She's decided to love him for the sum of his parts and cherish his overall value.

My dear friend is the luckiest girl in the world. I'm so proud to be her friend and the person that helped her recognize such a magical gift was already in her grasp.

Here's to holding on, never letting go, and to discovering our own fairy-tale beginning!

The Perfect Kiss

When you meet someone intriguing and agree to a first date, there's an incredible amount of promise and enthusiasm that goes along with the RSVP. It's the aftermath of the date, whether good or bad, that can leave you sad, heartbroken, lonely, and in some cases, discouraged. Personally, no matter the outcome, I continue to do it. Over and over again. I confess that sometimes the process of dating is exhausting. I sincerely believe that love should come naturally and with ease, like the perfect kiss.

Recently, I've been reminded of that innocent, yet intimate pleasure. It's complex in the fact that either person can ask for it, there's not one specific way to do it, and a chemical reaction happens, or it doesn't. Sometimes, the perfect kiss can happen with someone completely unexpected. (That's a real thrill!)

The perfect kiss can leave you wanting, breathless, and hopeful. It's a single moment of sheer bliss that captivates you and creates a memory that can last a lifetime; like a Santorini sunset. Depending upon the circumstance, the perfect kiss can be strong and overwhelming. The perfect kiss can be gentle, yet firm, and linger on your lips while making the hair on your arms stand up in excitement. The perfect kiss can leave you longing, eager, and even lightheaded, if initiated and delivered properly.

As my thirteen-year-old goddaughter said, "The perfect kiss must be in slow motion, but whatever you do, don't start off by slipping the tongue in first!" She continued to say that "the perfect kiss should leave you feeling like you've been swept off your feet." Sometimes the perfect kiss can be heated and overly dramatic, as described in a romance novel; like when a man grabs your shoulders from behind, brushes your hair to one shoulder, and whispers in your ear. Then, ever so seductively kisses your neck, with heat, passion, and romance, with a dash of the unexpected. What could be more romantic?

I think what some unfortunately overlook is that kissing is a very significant, intimate, highly sensual experience that can captivate hearts and minds forever.

I vividly remember my first kiss. It was innocent, meaningful, gentle, romantic, and courageous. I was about eight years old and living in Pascagoula, Mississippi. Teddy and I were on the playground during recess at Arlington Elementary School. Teddy kissed my hand. It was original and unforgettable.

As my quest for love continues twenty-plus first dates into the journey, I've realized that all kisses are not created equal. What I've learned is to kiss, and kiss often. Never lose the intimacy in kissing, or to negate its value. No matter your kissing preference—passionate, gentle, firm, or hair-pulling erotic—it's finding that unexpected connection with another person and the anticipation of the perfect kiss that makes all the bad dates worthwhile and keeps this single girl puckered up in Houston!

Break the Girl Code

Dating is hard enough, but let's add to the mix that cleverly designed social networking tool called Facebook. You have your profile page, a rolodex of friends, and then suddenly your friends become friends of your other friends. Think multi-level marketing! Do you realize what this has done, people? It's reducing our dating pool!

Girls have their rules and guys have their own rules. However, there's one rule that both sexes agree on: you don't date your friends' exes!

Dating Diva Dilemma: If you randomly become friends with someone via Facebook and are set up on a blind date only to find out that he dated one of your Facebook friends, what do you do? Do you still accept the date?

Keep in mind, you're not BFFs with the Facebook friend, but you never break girl code. It's disrespectful, and bad karma awaits you!!

What are your thoughts?

READER COMMENT FROM FACEBOOK:

I just came out and told her that I dated [Ms. X]. That's the best policy. I got that out of the way and it never became an issue.

I am so glad that I am married! Too many rules!

OK, this one is tricky. Do you only chat with this person on Facebook? I don't think it counts. Oh, I don't know. Maybe this is why I keep going back to my ex-boyfriend. Playing it safe!

I'm with the other guy—I couldn't do it! I'd be a bachelor the rest of my life.

The Dance

Throughout my quest for true love, I cannot seem to find fluidity in dating. The steps are unknown, and sudden dips are impossible to anticipate! The rules in baseball don't change from one field to the next, do they? No! So why do the rules of dating? What are the steps? How do I learn them?

At a young age, I remember watching my grandparents, William and Sue Brett, dance. It was an exquisite sight to behold as they drifted across the floor. I was in awe of their beauty, yet perplexed, because as they looked to be an unusual pairing under ordinary circumstances, they were a force of nature on the dance floor. Their chemistry was like watching fireworks at Disneyland. You couldn't help but smile as you were lit from within with joy. My grandmother shined as she looked at my grandfather. There was such admiration and trust as he led her across the dance floor. With poise and elegance, they moved as one. It was magical and my first glimpse at true love. One followed while the other led. The steps were well rehearsed and each knew the positions.

My grandparents have been married for over forty years. They've lived through the hardship of the Great Depression and war, raised twelve children, suffered extraordinary loss, and yet always found time to spend Saturday nights at "The Club" dancing. They've found joy, understanding, and complexity in the art of the dance.

Many years ago, my grandmother was diagnosed with Alzheimer's. She passed earlier this year. With each day, her memory faded and she drifted away. She couldn't recall our names, what she ate for lunch, or where she lived, but what's astounding is that she could remember all the steps in the dance.

I wonder if their relationship was so successful because one followed while the other led. Is marriage like a well-choreographed dance?

So let's look at this from a *Dancing with the Stars* perspective. You know the routine!

Step 1—Pairing Up

Dating is merely the "pairing up" phase; you're looking for a partner who not only complements your strengths, but also can encourage you to reach your full potential. Someone who will catch you when you fall yet will also let you fall and be there to help you stand up. (Some of us always learn lessons the hard way, including me!)

Step 2—Training

Anything worthwhile takes hard work, commitment, and time. Invest in yourself and your partner. Get prepared to work!

*Thirty-three-plus first dates and you'd think I'd be past step two!

Step 3—Understanding Your Partner

Each of us has strengths and weaknesses. In a partnership, self-improvement should be encouraged and fostered in a healthy, motivational manner. Understand, accept, and learn the art of compromise. In some instances, the choreography might change in order to enhance the overall pairing.

Step 4—Communication

Find healthy ways to discover, explore, and express yourself, which will then determine your pairings in choreography.

Step 5—Learn *Your* Choreography

What steps, lifts, or comedic charms work in some relationships might not be right for yours. Explore your partner and the possibilities. Enjoy!

Step 6—Vulnerability/Emotion

Allow yourself to become vulnerable and express yourself in the choreography. Allow yourself to need, trust, and rely on your partner.

Step 7—Dress Rehearsal

Costumes will malfunction, someone will fall, and steps will be forgotten. It's all about working through these obstacles together versus throwing in the towel.

Step 8—Performance of a Lifetime

Sizzle, sexuality, chemistry, and sheer brilliance—it is a performance of a lifetime!

One follows while the other leads. The steps are well rehearsed and each knows their position. May we all learn to "dance!"

Mr. and Mrs.

Contrary to popular belief, my adventures didn't recently begin. I've dated all types of men, and yet with such a stellar pool of candidates, I can't find the one who's right for me. What I can say with utter certainty is that I'm not looking for the following:

Father Time—This older gentleman is looking for a hot piece of arm candy and needs that little purple pill to help himself. Think J. Howard Marshall!

Daddy—This man will take care of you and make all decisions for you because you can't do anything for yourself. He views you as a "project" or a "work in progress." You are someone who he can mold into his perfect mate. Once perfected, he'll be off to his next "project."

The Gamer—This man will follow "The Rules," date three or four girls at a time, and enjoy the drama created by two girls in a catfight over him while acting as if he's done nothing wrong. He enjoys drama and playtime. Your emotions are like catnip to a feline. He'll drive you crazy!

The Party Guy—This guy is fun! You hop from one club to the next, greet everyone in the bar as if they're your best friends, and you always have a great time. The long-term challenge is: where's the substance?

The Mama's Boy—This man loves his mother to a fault. He will do anything and everything for her. Sometimes this is good, but when it comes time for your needs, are they being met? Are you being taken care of in this tug of war? Can he take care of himself, you, and potentially a family?

Disclaimer: A man should always love and respect his mother. He should respect his partner as well. Family first!

Mr. Baywatch—This man is looking to rescue a woman, any woman! He finds joy and fulfillment in correcting the problem. (If only Jason Statham were a lifeguard. He could rescue and "transport" me anywhere!)

Mr. Identity—This man wraps his entire existence around "things." That is, his car, boat, work, country club, and his portfolio. Enough said!

Mr. Metro—This man dresses like he's from Los Angeles. He wears square-toed shoes, adorns himself with John Hardy jewelry, and takes more time to get ready than you do. These guys typically use more Paul Mitchell hair gel than Sephora has in stock!

Caution: Running your hands through this guy's hair will cause permanent scarring and frequent trips to the nail salon!

Mr. WTF—This man constantly complains about everything and it's always someone else's fault. He talks so much that you should be paid hourly for your services. He never asks you about "you." So in the end, you're left with WTF!

Mr. Unbelievable—This man will buy you a great condo, pay for your monthly living expenses, and provide an open charge for you at La Perla. He'll lavish you with diamonds, sapphires, and Birkins. The only problem is, you'll eventually find out that you're one of three in his "collection."

Mr. Meathead—This man is consumed with his biceps more than his brain. He's a steroid freak and wants you to "stick him" in his posterior daily! He's got a hot body until you discover that some muscles are bigger than others. What a loss. Give me brains versus the brawn!

Mr. Confused—Let's just say that one minute you're at dinner, and the next, he's staring at another man with much affection. He'll take a trip to Amsterdam, only to return home to have had a threesome with others of the same gender. (Yes, I've encountered him too!)

Mr. Controlling—He'll slowly but surely limit access to your friends, family, and activities, and put the kibosh on your personal goals. You'll find him going through your Blackberry, voicemail, and text messages. He'll reveal his true colors in time, but it's already too late. He'll consume your life and ultimately control you. Once you've been captured, let the extreme makeover begin. Think *Enough* or *Sleeping With the Enemy*.

Mr. Perfect—This man seeks ultimate perfection in himself and his partner. This isn't necessarily a bad thing as long as you realize that perfection doesn't truly exist. (Well, maybe in a Texas sunset!) This man is an advocate for any form of plastic surgery and will readily tell you what you need, as his hairline—what hairline?

Mr. Right Now—This man only lives for today. He savors the moment while not looking for anything long-term. He treats you well, and you believe that there's potential. He is the quintessential bachelor. He's a man with his own plan, and it's not inclusive of a partner but rather someone to enjoy spending time with. Think George Clooney!

So do you want to know what I'm looking for? It's fairly simple!

Mr. and Mrs.—They respect one another's dreams while encouraging them, communicate, enjoy sex, are adventurous and multi-dimensional, trusting, easy to be around, don't play games, are respectful of one another's quirks, can be goofy, reliable, loving, nurturing, and family-oriented. They enjoy the country, city, travel, and all that life has to offer.

Find laughter in the adventure that lies within the quest for true love. I hope we find joy, learn about ourselves, understand what we'll compromise, identify what we need versus what we want, and ultimately find a greater appreciation for our Mr. and Mrs.!

READER COMMENT FROM FACEBOOK:

Sometimes I think the comments are the best part. Just enjoy her writing, people. Comment on it and share your thoughts, but please don't take it too seriously. Lori comes across to me as someone who knows what she's looking for, and it's not Mr. Perfect. She's looking for Mr. Real. A man who appreciates her brains as much as her beauty, her quirks as much as her style, and her faults as much as her strengths. It's what every mature woman who has the luxury of choice would prefer in a man.

The sad truth is that a great majority of single men out there are simply not what she's looking for. Most of the real men she's looking for are already content or blissfully happy with their own wives and families.

Good luck finding your Mr. Diva, Lori. As with all of us looking for true love, you'll need all the luck you can get. But, whatever you do, keep on not settling. He's out there looking for you.

Let's Hear It for the Men

A dear friend requested that I write a brief article listing positive things about men. I agreed to do it, but I hope that you believe this isn't fiction material!

- A man is strong and you can rest your head on his shoulders while watching a movie.

- When a man cuddles with you as you sleep, it's the most intimate and loving feeling in the world.

- A man is super sexy when he shaves in the morning.

- A man sweats—that's sexy!

- A man smells good!

- A man makes you feel safe and protected just by being in your presence.

- A man makes you feel like a woman and how!

- A man is really sexxy* when doing manly stuff, like yard work, replacing a light bulb, playing football, or working on the ranch.

- A man appreciates your leather and lace collection! (But doesn't wear it!)

- A man knows how to press you against a wall and kiss you like he means it!

- When a man cares about you, you'll never doubt where you stand in his world.

- When a man really loves, he loves deeper than a woman.

---

* Yes, double *x* for extra hottie!

Hope this makes all the beautiful, sexy men out there feel appreciated today!

READER COMMENT FROM FACEBOOK:

The last two on your list really took me by surprise. I am pleasantly surprised that at least one woman understands those truths and is sharing it with others who may not. Those two positives about men go hand-in-hand and can help create either a deeply profound love between two people or one helluva frustrated woman who is unsuccessfully trying to find love with a man who does not exhibit those positives with her. The quicker a woman realizes that she is in a relationship characterized by the latter, the sooner she can get out and find a man who wants to be with her and create the former. The flip side is that men should also understand those two positives about themselves so they can be on the lookout for a woman with whom they can revel in the true love experience. So many people settle for so much less; it's no wonder our divorce rate is so high.

Dodgeball, Anyone?

Over the past several weeks, I've had the surreal experience of meeting some incredibly loyal readers. These enthusiastic moments have brought me tremendous joy, and yet, can be a little overwhelming, too. These encounters have given me the opportunity to learn more about you (our readers) and your dating experiences. I find it flattering that some feel unusually comfortable sharing such personal, love-related experiences. (Yes, I'm referring to you, leather and lace!) Having said that, I must "tip my hat" and say thank you! Now, there have been a couple of moments when I felt battered and bruised because of my Dating Diva Adventures. Let's just say that for safety's sake, I'm still wearing my protective gear! Understand that it may appear easy to bear your soul to over two thousand readers and share your innermost thoughts about love, sex, and relationships, but try it—you'll feel like you're the last person left standing in a game of dodgeball while everyone takes aim at you! Did you cringe just thinking about it? Do you remember that feeling? You know the balls are coming, you just pray that when one hits you, and eventually one will, that it doesn't hurt too badly.

As for me, playing this strategic game of dodgeball (a.k.a. dating) has been liberating. I've finally found my voice and I'm no longer ashamed to say what I need or want in a relationship. Writing this book and my column has been beyond therapeutic. It's provided an outlet for self-expression that, until now, has always been foreign to me. What's brought me a genuine sense of peace is that I believed I was alone in the quest for true love. Thanks to your e-mails and introductions, I've learned that I was never alone. There are so many of us believers in true love. (Wow, it almost sounds like a cult, eh?) The irony is that in this process of unveiling my heart's desire, I feel naked when meeting people now. Bearing your soul and allowing others to accept it or reject it is terrifying! Don't misunderstand me—it stings like a dodgeball smashing into your forehead when you're rejected. You're left with some memory loss and minor abrasions. But eventually, you recover! Bottom line—I've learned to let it all hang out and just reject the fear. The heart does heal, and every time I have a misadventure, I grow stronger, but only when I allow myself to be vulnerable; like when I'm waiting for a dodgeball to smack into me!

Wishing you a limited amount of memory loss during your next game of dodgeball!

P.S. Anyone got an ice pack? My head is killing me!

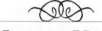

Mars to Venus

Listen up, divas! I'm here to say that there are members of the opposite sex all over the United States who are writing in and curious about the quest for true love. While on this spectacular odyssey, I never imagined that so many would appreciate the out-of-this-world candor, or relate to my dating dilemmas, for that matter. What's fascinating is that these men not the type who linger too long, would be considered overly needy, or talk about the latest *Star Wars* movies. (Thank goodness!) These are charming, educated, single, quality men that are looking for their true love, just like us! However, these men have questions! They're trying to uncover that black hole of a mystery behind what women need! So sit back, adjust your five-point safety harness, and get ready for liftoff! This flight is going from Mars to Venus!

Dating Diva 1
What makes a great first date?

Have a plan and then share that plan. It must involve one-on-one time. No group dates, please! You truly would not have time to get to know one another. Select a venue that allows for relaxing conversation versus a techno-thumping, overly crowded restaurant where you're forced to raise your voice to speak to one another. No "twenty questions," either. This is not a game show. Talk about the day's events. No one likes to be interviewed, especially in this economy. Think simplicity! Memorial Park, Discovery Green, an art festival, or walking the beach in Galveston.

Suggestion: no road trips on a first date! You don't want to be calling a car service, or something far worse, the police, if it suddenly goes wrong.

Dating Diva 2

What makes a great first kiss?

Wow! This differs for everyone. For me, it's about the anticipation of it, then waiting for his lips to touch mine, while not having the patience to wait any longer.

Dating Diva 3

What do you notice first about a guy?

When he says something intelligent! You can be mouthwateringly, Carter Oosterhouse–hot, but please, have something to back it up with. Captivate me mentally, and then you'll captivate me physically. Grrr!

Dating Diva 4

What makes a great first night over?

Not planning for it! Romance—sex—should happen naturally and not be planned or expected. If you think you're getting lucky, have things that might make us feel more comfortable, like our favorite drink, a toothbrush, or give us your shirt to sleep in. We love that because it smells like you. Very sexy!

Suggestion: whatever you do, guys, have toilet paper!

Dating Diva 5

What is the most common mistake guys make?

Honestly, I haven't experienced any "common mistakes." For me, you either have chemistry or you don't. You make time for the other person, or you don't. You make the decision to call, or you don't. If a man is interested, I'll know by the way he treats me. He'll know if I'm interested by the way I look at him.

Dating Diva 6

What do you wish we knew that we don't?

We want to be cared for, our love cherished. We like being treated like a princess in the manner that you treat us and not by what you buy us. We want to feel safe in your presence and know that it's all right to let our guard down. We want to be assured that we don't have to be Wonder Woman, just a Super Woman in your eyes, as those are the only eyes that matter to us.

Dating Diva 7

How do we know when you want us to just listen as opposed to fix the problem?

When you listen to us, believe it or not, it shows you care. This somehow represents friendship and love in our minds. (Maybe that's just me, though.) Sometimes it's not about the problem; it's the simple fact that you're there for us. Everyone needs help, and at times, we're too proud to ask. So be direct and ask us.

Again, I'm not the shuttle commander! I do not have all the answers. I merely have my own intergalactic, starry-eyed, romantic notions. With that said, I'd like ask my fellow divas to share their thoughts!

READER COMMENT FROM FACEBOOK:

Well, I'm no diva, but I generally have an opinion I like to share. I think that men who claim they don't understand women are either not trying hard enough or living in denial. Women generally make it clear about how they feel, and if the man is really, truly listening and engages in the discussions, then he will get it and understand her better. Since not all women are the same, this listening thing is fairly important. However, sometimes men just don't want to accept what she is saying (denial) because it may mean he has to give up more of his lifestyle or relinquish more control than he is willing to. For those guys, it's easier to claim they don't understand women than it is to accept the need for change.

Easy Target

There comes a time in every single girl's life when she screams at the top of her lungs, "Enough, already!" I've wondered, is there a freaking sign on my forehead that only men can see? "Easy Target." I mean, really, I'm perplexed here!

Many years ago, I met a thriller of a man. We dated for a month or so. I was enchanted with him, and the chemistry was undeniable. Truly, I thought we were headed for something spectacular. One day over lunch, he explained to me that he had been talking to his ex-girlfriend, and they had decided to work things out. OK, this was just brutal news! I was clearly shattered, as the tears cascaded down my cheeks. How disappointing and embarrassing! Although devastated, I was impressed that he was honest about his feelings and told me directly versus over an e-mail or not at all. He behaved like a man, and although I was upset, I appreciated the friendship and respect that he had shown me. In my opinion, that took courage on his part and should be recognized.

Now, I truly believe that there's a purpose for every person who crosses our path in life. There's a lesson in each encounter. The path that you choose and what you take away from it, well, that's up to you! As for Mr. Thriller and me, our paths cross in the most unusual of places, from the streets of New York City to a posh cafe in Los Angeles. Typically, we cross paths when I'm happily in a relationship. I'm sure you can relate! Recently, our paths have crossed again via a text message.

Mr. Thriller: Is this still your cell number?

Dating Diva: Yes

Mr. Thriller: How r u?

Dating Diva: Pretty good. I saw you about 2 weeks ago. Sunday, Escalante's. You were at valet.

Mr. Thriller: Coffee?

Dating Diva: Sweetie, you're married. That's probably not a great idea.

(Yes, he married the girl he dumped me for, his ex.)

Mr. Thriller: Wrong impression, I think. No worries. Hope u r well.

Dating Diva: What am I missing then? Tell me. Wasn't trying to be assumptive but …

Mr. Thriller: No worries. Will ping you later on in the week.

Frankly, there's nothing perplexing about this, unless I'm truly a complete idiot! The lesson is so simple. Stop communicating with and falling for unavailable men! I will no longer repeat the same mistakes. I will no longer be an easy target! Instead, I'm going to be my own personal cupid with a modern-day bow and arrow. (i.e. *Dating Diva Adventures*) By acknowledging my dating patterns, I feel empowered now. Suddenly, I'm able to admit to myself the type of relationship that I'm genuinely searching for. It will be a relationship that I'll respect and one that I deserve. I've taken control of my love life, which means it's open season, and I'm ready for target practice, boys, as this Cupid is taking aim! Here's to the quest for true love and to no longer being the fool!

Your E-mails Addressed

What a difference a day makes! I can only say that I've received about thirty-five e-mails today regarding *Dating Diva Adventures*. If I may, I'd like to address them in this manner.

The Journey:

My journey isn't about marriage. My journey is about finding true love. My journey is about caring for someone else more than I do for myself. Loving someone so deeply than I ache without him and cannot wait to wake up in the morning just to roll over and speak with him. My journey is about wanting to live my life and share my life with someone else. I believe wholeheartedly that this type of love exists. Don't you?

The Marriage:

I was married for seven years to a very loving, compassionate, and wonderful man who I admired tremendously. The issue was that he loved me more than I loved him. I loved him like a friend and not how a wife should love her husband. He deserved better than I could give him. I needed to know if true love, deep love, existed, and so I made the most difficult decision of my life—to divorce a wonderful man! Yes, I'm a stupid girl! If I had wanted "things" and security, I would've stayed married. So please, do not think for one moment that this is about materialism. That one stung. Neosporin, please!

Without the divorce, I would've never met Jean Paul, so read the chapter about "Great Love" for a better understanding!

The Article:

Now about "Mr. and Mrs.," it is apparent that I have provoked a few non-comedic-type readers! My point is that the "Mrs." are individuals who I'm not looking for. However, for every one of those

"Mrs.," there is a "Mrs." that matches him perfectly. Make sense? Women are far from perfect! Have you seen us when we wake up in the morning? We are hot messes!

My personal ideal "Mr. and Mrs." is described at the bottom of that article. I believe that this relationship is possible between a man and a woman. I believe because I've seen it and had it before. I believe in the impossible. Great things do not happen on their own; you must work toward them and invest in them. I'm willing to wear my heart on my sleeve in this book-writing process so that I can never regret not striving for the impossible. Cheer me on in this process as I am doing this for every Lifetime movie of the week viewer out there!

The Blame:

Disagreements will happen in a relationship. Is it ever any one person's fault? Goodness, no! I'm looking for what's right for me. No one knows what's right for me better than I do. Just because someone isn't right for me doesn't mean that there's anything wrong with that person at all. Some people, no matter how fabulous, are just not compatible.

The Dating Diva:

Some articles aren't totally about *my* dating experience but do include tidbits from my girlfriends' experiences.

The Laughter and Irritation:

Sometimes when writing, I have to make people laugh and provoke them as well. It cannot all be fairy-tale land! It's all for the sake of the book, fan base, and marketing plan! It's all about poking good fun at a subject matter that every single girl talks about! Laugh! Enjoy the ride, and if you're married to your Mr. Perfect, go hug him!

The Quest for True Love:

I believe in love and I believe that I will find the right person for me—one who will love me for all of my imperfections!

Thank you so very much for all of your e-mails! You have no idea how much I appreciate your insights to dating and relationships, and your stories about your one true love that you've so generously shared with me! Wow, what a difference a day makes!

All about the Benjamins

Warning: this article is not for the faint of heart. You will experience sudden detours ahead. Follow the signs, be cautious, and buckle up for safety, because it's all about the Benjamins.

If you're truly an avid follower of the "Adventures," you'd recall that when I began writing my column, I explained that I had been writing a book about first dates on Match.com. I mentioned that there's an enormous amount of self-discovery and mental exhaustion associated with this endeavor and especially with this subject! Now with fabulous friends assisting in the dating selection process, it's been challenging. Everyone has had their own opinions about who I should date and why I should date them! (Shocking, eh? Women with opinions.) On more than one occasion, there's been a question raised, and it's not an easy one to address. However, I must confront the subject head-on as it's too juicy to walk away from! This subject is far from politically correct, so again, put your protective gear on and let the controversy begin!

Would you date someone who earns less money than you? Specifically, would you date someone who earns half of what you do?

From my perspective, and please let your own moral compass be your guide, if the person is everything you dreamed of and has a career on the horizon, goals, education, dreams, and the initiative to make things happen, of course, without question—go for it!

Here's where it gets tricky—if the person is older and settled in their career and earns a significant amount less than you, do you still date him? Is it possible that there will there come a point in the relationship where you lose respect for the other person? When you're consistently the primary breadwinner, will you become disgruntled over time because he or she can't afford to dine at restaurants that you frequent? Participate in the same hobbies that you enjoy? Go on weekend trips that you're accustomed to? Contribute to the dream house that you both desire? Would you be making the other feel bad because he or she cannot afford to do the same things that you like to do? As a woman, you'd never be able to quit your job, be a stay at home mom, and raise your children, because you're the primary breadwinner. Now, breathe—I can feel the daggers coming my way!

The answer is—drum roll, please—I don't have the answer for *you*! I only have the answer for *me*!

When I flash back to some of my most memorable dates (thank you, Nebraska), not one of them had anything to do with money, location, my hobbies, or restaurants. They had to do with the person, conversation, laughter, and overall chemistry. Over time, I've learned that the things that make me the most happy are good friends, simplicity, and being outdoors. None of which have anything to do with money. If I'm lucky enough to meet a phenomenal person and one with an open heart like mine, I guarantee that we'll find things to do together that we enjoy because we're together. If the relationship blossoms into something greater and children are part of our equation, one of us could stay at home. Believe it or not, there are stellar, stay at home dads! I've learned that money does not buy happiness. I'll take a loving, loyal, trusting, hardworking, driven man that has time for me over a black American Express card any day of the week. Money doesn't keep you warm at night! I've learned that money can sometimes alienate you from the reality of life, family, and your real friends, too.

My advice is simple; do what's right for you. Follow your heart, and when in doubt, ask questions, communicate with your partner, and discuss your money concerns. In the end, if you're meant to be together, you'll find a path that's right for the both of you. I guarantee, or your money back. It won't have anything to do with Benjamins.

All about the Benjamins—Part 2

I received this e-mail from a loyal and charming reader. After digesting it, I thought, *Why not give my fellow dating divas an opportunity to contribute to the conversation?* The topic is sensational, juicy, and beyond politically incorrect. Love it!

Ladies, let's provide some classy, yet sassy, real-world answers. Are you ready? Let's continue.

Dear Dating Diva:

I read your column, "All about the Benjamins," and it pretty much hit the nail on the head. This is a messy subject with no easy answers, which seems to get more complicated as we get older and inevitably encounter greater disparities in financial success. In your case, you're looking for true love, so you value the intangibles (e.g. it's the thought that counts and the little things that matter). I'm in the same place and in agreement, yet—I'm sure you'd agree—there are financial realities that will test a relationship. It's one thing for a couple who marries early—like my parents—to start with nothing and have to deal with financial adversity. It's another to be dealing with this when you're in your forties. The challenge is how do you screen for gold diggers and avoid the prostitution-type model of dating? Or how do you avoid a variation on this theme, namely that you become a convenient meal ticket and ego boost while your date has no interest in a real relationship? When do chivalry and generosity cross the line into being a sucker?

The latter is what I discovered in my recent dating experience which lasted about six weeks. Despite chemistry, long effortless conversations, and having a great deal in common, there were plenty of red flags. Yet she was masterful at keeping me at the poker table; getting me to throw more money in the pot just to turn over another card. The final call to her upping the ante was a four-day weekend in California. (Having recently moved to Texas, she owns a high-rise apartment in California which she needed to rent out.) Despite one of her girlfriends visiting, she assured me we'd spend plenty of time together. Long story short, the weekend was a series of broken plans and [had] me constantly biting my lip, compromising, and going with the flow to make everyone happy. On Sunday (after breaking plans once again), the two of us and her friend drove up the coast. Despite my frustration with not getting any alone time, I did my best to make sure her friend was happy and comfortable. As it turned out, we all had a great day. Unfortunately, we didn't get back to California until 8:00 PM. She informed her friend that we needed to spend some alone time (finally!) and that she would take me to one of her favorite spots for dessert. Then an awkward moment came up. I truly expected her to pay for dessert (up to that point I had paid for virtually everything), yet she asked me for money. She then said I should not only pay for her, but also her friend. That one floored me. (BTW, this girlfriend is a thirty-five-year-old employed lawyer.) Further, she said her guy friends always paid her way. My comment was that I didn't always pay for my platonic girlfriends, though that didn't mean it was necessarily fifty-fifty. As it turned out, these guys all wanted to date her (or were ex-boyfriends), which I said was just wrong in my book.

Of course, I didn't mind paying, but I did feel totally used. Any thoughts on how often and how much the woman should contribute to the dating budget? And how do I protect myself in the future? I suppose one way is to make sure the relationship is reciprocating (though not necessarily money) and back away at the first sign that it isn't. It's not like I'm swimming in money, but should I continue to keep a low profile and live well below my means to avoid attracting the wrong type? When does frugality cross the line into poor marketing and date repellant?

Signed,

Monetarily Confused

Dear Monetarily Confused:

When you feel like you're being taken advantage of, you most likely are! When a woman cares for you, you'll know it by the way she looks at you, treats you, and respects your needs, as well as her own. If you're not getting what you need out of a relationship, move on. There are lots of beautiful, intelligent, single women in the fantastic state of Texas who would appreciate a man as articulate, charming, and as thoughtful as you. Always trust and respect yourself, because if you don't, she won't, either.

READER COMMENT FROM FACEBOOK:

I completely agree with your assessment of this subject. Since there aren't any other ladies commenting on this, I will share my own opinion.

My comment to Monetarily Confused is that this is a hard subject to deal with and certainly requires an objective approach with each lady he dates. Yes, I said objective approach. That is, step back and look at the clues and statements she gives from a third-person perspective. If you don't do that but instead rely on your subjective viewpoint, you'll too easily convince yourself that the cues she's giving aren't really indicative of her feelings or her nature. Along with this comes the requirement of a touch of realism. Denial is an ugly beast, and as long as you feed it, it will hang around and you'll never know the truth until the beast takes a bite out of you.

Chemistry? Long conversations? They sound nice (and required, of course), but he left out the red flags he alluded to. What were they, exactly? I would venture to guess that the red flags, when perceived through an objective lens, would make the chemistry a bit explosive.

I'm going to guess this lady was quite the looker. As the Dating Diva said, there are plenty of beautiful and intelligent women in Houston that will appreciate Monetarily Confused. But, even more importantly, many of those women understand and follow the Golden Rule. Learning whether a lady you date has these qualities is quite simple when you have effortless conversations and actually listen to what she says.

The Geography of Dating

Recently, while enjoying a girls night out sponsored by Belvedere Vodka and Moet Chandon, I engaged in a discussion around "The Geography of Dating." Admittedly so, I have more experience than most in this department. Cue the "stab in the heart" motion! As the conversation progressed, I was asked, "Have you noticed a difference in the way men approach you depending on where they are from? Is there a difference in methods used to get to know you or romance you during the dating process?" This left me wondering—could it be possible that we're looking for love in the wrong hemisphere? Is it time to renew the passport and book a flight to Rome after all? Whoa, not so fast! Don't start packing the monogrammed Louis Vuitton, ladies!

I've had the good fortune to reside in thirteen different states, work as a flight attendant, and enjoy a long-time career that has afforded me the luxury of travel. I've dated men from Argentina, Australia, England, Jordan, France, Italy, Syria, Venezuela, Pakistan, and the great United States of America! Men with careers that range from professional athlete, actor, model, photographer, doctor, investment banker, attorney, executive, pilot, and so on. The bottom line is this: I've had a good cross section of data to analyze!

Truly, I'd never considered "The Geography of Dating." Utterly intriguing! The more I began to ponder it and the more champagne I consumed, I was surprisingly provided with a unique moment of clarity.

Family and Culture:

While almost everyone professes that family is of utmost importance, I found a great appreciation for other cultures and the commitment to family. I appreciated meeting family members early on in the dating process. Inevitably, you not only marry the man, you marry into the family. Who wants to spend your entire life arguing with in-laws? Respect and understanding for other cultures is critical. Learning about other cultures versus assuming, or quoting an *NCIS* episode, is not appropriate. Educate yourself, as it shows you're interested in the person you're dating and in your own self-improvement! (Stop poking fun at someone's accent and slang terms. It's belittling to you.) I discovered that unlike American culture, some must marry within their own culture. This made it increasingly difficult, and I was forced to make decisions early on in dating.

Dating Diva Scenario:

While in college and living in New York, my good friend Anna dated a man for two years. Due to the fact that she wasn't of his religion, she wasn't accepted into the family. She thought his family members would change their minds over time. Unfortunately, they broke up. Not even three months later, he was engaged to another and soon after, married! The heartbreak was devastating. After this experience, I could never invest myself in a relationship knowing the fatal outcome, nor would I change my religious beliefs for the sake of love or marriage.

Romance:

Romance differs in each relationship, but in some ways, always remains the same. It is meaningful in all the ways that truly matter. Sometimes it's the landscape that provides the romance. Trust me, I know! The Plaza Athenee is not my permanent residence. I've already tried forwarding my mail. Ugh, "Return to Sender." Yes, it's a shocker! My experience is that romance can be in the architecture, a Buenos Aries sunset, the smell of the flowers in the South of France, taste of the freshest carpaccio with provolone, roar of the subway car, or simply in escaping your everyday routine and experiencing something new as a couple. Yes, the French, Latinos, and Italians have the accents and joie de vivre, but any romantic relationship takes two. Enjoy it all and be grateful for the romance in your every day! Reality versus fantasy, right? Unless you're a cast member from *The Bachelorette*!

Geography:

I found Northeastern men to be more businesslike and less emotionally in tune with themselves. They tend to be very well-educated, speak more about international news than local, and focus on climbing the corporate ladder versus living. They treat you very well and adore their family!

I found that West Coast men are more outdoor oriented, emotionally available and able to talk about their feelings, open to new experiences, yet very interested in physical appearance. Understandably so—have you seen *Dr. 90210*? Ouch!

Some Southern men are stellar at romancing you, but once they "land" you, you suddenly turn into a housewife while they tune into NASCAR, and you're left popping the top on a cold can of beer.

I could ramble on, but the end result is that the United States is a melting pot of many religions, cultures, languages, and traditions, all of which are beautiful. We should respect them and learn about them, and maybe we'll find that special someone just by allowing ourselves to live, love, and not overanalyze the unique beauty in others. So put on your Chanel lip gloss, throw on your Manolos, grab your Louis Vuitton luggage, and I'll meet you at the airport. You've just renewed your passport to love!

Sometimes Sex Is Just Sex

I've tried to avoid this subject as it could be considered less than ladylike to discuss. However, I've recently discovered that some of my fellow divas are rather inexperienced or clueless when it comes to dating and sex. For the record, I was confused too. Then, I began my quest for love and, along with three of my fabulous friends, analyzed my own personal dating habits, blunders, and faux pas! The outcome was worth the extreme humiliation and degradation. However, I recommend doing this exercise with a bottle of Dom Pérignon! It seems to make everything more palatable, right?

When you start dating someone, take the time to get to know them. If you truly want a long lasting and tangible relationship, do not jump into a sexual relationship! Men are simple creatures. They want sex! They need sex! When they say, "You look gorgeous," "your eyes are beautiful," or "I love that dress," they mean, "I want to have sex with you." (Guyroglyphics—get familiar with them!) Yes, they mean it, because we're all fabulous, but ultimately, that's what they're thinking! We (women) are so easily manipulated and desperately seek the approval of a man. Why? Daddy issues maybe, I don't know!

We believe that we'll find the love of our lives by giving ourselves so freely—both mentally and physically—while all along some guys are just playing us like pawns on a chessboard. Actions speak louder than words. Trust me, I know! I realized that if I had paid closer attention and stopped creating my dream man instead of truly seeing what was in front of me, I wouldn't have wasted so much valuable time. In the end, the man I thought was my Prince Charming didn't exist. I created him, while the man left standing in front of me was foreign. I didn't know who he was, nor did I care to know. Ah, you live and you learn. My point is that I speak from experience and I would never wish my experience on anyone else. Ladies, try this. Take your time. Enjoy being treated like the class act that you are. Let a man chase you. It's like when you're hunting; if you chase a wild animal, it will run away from you! Stop chasing the man. Make sense?

No one values anything that comes easily or is readily available, right? Don't you want that limited edition Chanel handbag that's so elusive? Of course you do! That's what a man wants in a woman. Get to know a man. Listen as much as you talk.

Allow him to make the evening plans and open your eyes to the real man, not the fantasy man that you've created when you met him initially. Learn about him. We're so wrapped up in talking about ourselves and selling ourselves that we overlook the simple truth—he might not be so fabulous for us! There are men that merely tell you what you want to hear and do just exactly what they need to in order to get you in the sack. I know, it's an epiphany, right? Now, if you're just looking for a great time, OK! I'm open-minded to the concept that sometimes sex is just sex. Sometimes great sex is just great sex! Do not confuse great sex with love, though. Those are two completely different animals, ladies! Although, I do not advise unsafe sex. Protect yourself and your future. Let's agree to take control while slowing down the dating process and really get to know the person who we're going out with. If you genuinely like him, take the time to get to know him and stop this insanity. Stop asking, "Why hasn't he called after four dates?" after you had sex on the third date. Be smart and realize that real men exist and are looking for a potential partner. They want to connect with someone on a mental and emotional level, while building a solid foundation during the dating process. Slow down, take your time, invest in yourself and in the relationship, and enjoy the process of dating, because if you don't, to a man, sometimes sex is just sex!

The One That Got Away

It was a scorching summer day like most in New York City. As I began my morning walk to the trendy Northern Italian eatery where I worked, Canastel's, on the Eastside, I could tell that day was different. There was something about the city that felt refreshed and invigorated. For those of you familiar with the city, you'd know that it has a buzz about it. It has an energy that is undeniable. You feel it in your core. It revives you and is intoxicating, and can be like a much needed fix to an addict. Maybe it was the hope of the invitation to Marc's house in the Hamptons for the weekend, I don't know. Nevertheless, it was going to be memorable. I just knew it!

I arrived at work and my shift began like any other. I set up my tables and made sure that my section was pristine. You never knew who would dine at the restaurant from the William Morris Agency on any given day. So you had to make certain that you were on your A-game as every little detail mattered. It was a show, although truly, it was just lunch. Every girl who worked at this well-known establishment was selected because of their model-like looks and each was unique, yet blended with the rest of the staff. I say this because I certainly wasn't hired for my wait skills but due to the fact that I fit the uniform and demographic profile. At this age, who cared about profiling, as long as the tips were fierce and I had the opportunity to meet potential agents, celebrities, actors, or producers. Every day I entered the restaurant, I hoped that this day could be my big break and I could be discovered!

Canastel's was the place to be! From the Knicks, Stallone, OJ Simpson, Nicole Brown-Simpson, Heather Locklear, Milla Jovovich, super model and face of Estée Lauder Paulina, and her husband Rick from the Cars, Lawrence Taylor, Geraldo Rivera, Donald Trump, and the list goes on! They've all dined at Canastel's, and I've had the pleasure of waiting on them.

As I hustled about the floor and fought my way to the register, Claudia, one of my coworkers and friend from Rio, told me of a man who was sitting in her section who wanted to meet me. I explained to her that I was in the weeds and just picked up more tables because the other waitress couldn't handle her own section. I told her to politely explain to her customer the situation, and if I could, I'd gladly stop by later.

Understand the restaurant capacity is 250 persons, and when full, you cannot see from one end to the other. Basically, I didn't have the ability to glance over and see this mystery man.

The shift was exhausting, but my charms were in full force as Mr. Morgan Freeman was dining in my section and celebrating his anniversary with his lovely wife. What a fine actor! Might I add a true class act! I was passively alert and focused on the table, when out of the blue, Claudia approached with this 6'3", blond, blue-eyed, surfer-type man with a tan that was courtesy of the West Coast! This surfer boy was literally tied up with rope that Claudia was holding. She then proceeded to tie the loose end to the banister in my section. Absolutely clueless to whom was behind me—Mr. and Mrs. Morgan Freeman—this surfer boy explained that he would not leave my section until I agreed to have dinner with him that evening. Increasingly, his tone elevated, and I could feel my boss, Marcello, racing across the floor to reach my section. Without haste, I agreed, "Yes, I'll go out with you!" As I begged Claudia to remove Surfer Boy, I could see Mr. and Mrs. Freeman grinning from ear to ear. As it was their own romantic day, I believed they saw the uniqueness of Surfer Boy's approach. If the Freemans approved, so be it!

At 10:00 PM that evening, we had agreed to meet back at the restaurant and then decide where to venture for dinner. As we began walking Park Avenue South, I realized how nervous Surfer Boy appeared. It was rather endearing, so I tried my best to make him laugh. The hope was that it would ease the pressure of the initial "getting to know you." Surfer Boy told me that he was an apprentice photographer here on assignment for the next three days. His client was a land development company. He explained that he was basically gathering images of sites and buildings. As the walk continued, I learned that he was an avid rock-climber, surfer, snowboarder, and adventure thrill-seeker. At this point in my life, I'd never met anyone like him. Even to this day, he's one of the most fascinating people I've encountered. We stumbled across this Thai restaurant that seemed appealing to us both. I had never tried Thai food before, so what the heck! This could be fun, right? Surfer Boy was incredibly charming and explained everything on the menu. Again, I had never experienced Thai food, so this was necessary! We established my allergy to ginger, so he communicated this to the waiter, and the adventure began. Who knew that the newness of a person combined with that of food could be so mysterious and sexy? We dined for about three-and-a-half hours. He was emotional, eloquent, sincere, passionate, strong, and humble. Words do not do Surfer Boy justice! The night was young; it was only 1:30 AM. We decided to go to a little bar around the corner, and later ended up walking around the city until nearly sunrise. We got back to my place and my roommate was upstairs, sound asleep. I was feeling comfortable with him, so I allowed him inside the apartment to use the facilities. As I was sitting on the couch, he sat next to me, and that's the last thing I can remember until we woke up the next morning! We had fallen asleep sitting straight up on the sofa. Talk about a neck ache! He realized what time it was and rushed out the door. Without a kiss good-bye or even an "I'll call you later," Surfer Boy was gone. I was left feeling rather dizzy (maybe hung over is a better term) and confused, so I grabbed some ibuprofen, headed upstairs, and crawled into bed. After all, this is New York. You meet people randomly. They enter your life as quickly as they exit. It's a revolving door of adventure.

You just have to be willing to accept it while not taking it personally. Sometimes it's about being a great dinner companion, tour guide, or maybe, could it be, a bad date. Yes, I said it. Maybe I was just a horrid date. It is possible!

I woke up about 2:00 PM. Instantly, I consumed two cups of coffee before going for my run. As I was pounding the pavement, I was getting really irritated and wondering what had happened! In the back of my mind, I knew that it was just timing. It had to be. As I recalled our conversation from earlier, I remembered he still had one more night in the city, so I secretly hoped that I'd see him later.

That night, it was back to work, and the evening shift was in full gear. It was packed, as always, and my section was slamming. As usual, the Gypsy Kings and The Doors are pumping. Out of the corner of my eye, I could see these long-stemmed, red roses approaching. I figured I had better dodge them before I got knocked down. The delivery must be for a patron. Suddenly, from behind the massive roses, I saw him. It was Surfer Boy! Wow, this guy knew how to get my attention! Was this a California thing, or was he just this good? He offered the roses and proceeded to apologize for leaving so quickly that morning, and said he hoped that I would go out with him after my shift. I agreed, and so did the other five girls gathered around us! Lemon has some explaining to do!

I finished my shift, cleaned up, and was ready for a night on the town. We decided to keep it simple and head toward Union Square and SoHo. While walking, we approached a diner. Understand, there's one on nearly every corner. We slipped inside and ate quickly before agreeing to check out a new club. As I sat across the table, I could tell there was something special about this guy, but I just wasn't sure I wanted to get romantically involved. He would be leaving to return to California in fourteen hours. Yes, he comes to New York once a month for business, but I'm young, no ties to anyone, and I like being single! I decided to play it cool and just relax. Why do women always have to think ten steps ahead when dating? Why can't we just enjoy the moment? So with these questions in mind, I decided to just relax. Later, we hit the club and danced the night away!

At 6:00 AM, our time together had come to an end. I needed some sleep as I had a casting call at 10:00 AM, and he had a plane to catch. We agreed to keep in touch, and he wrote me as often as possible. A simple kiss goodnight, along with a beautiful embrace, and that was the end of my Surfer Boy adventure. Or so I thought.

About two weeks had passed with no word from Surfer Boy, but then a letter arrived. I opened the letter and could not believe my eyes! Surfer Boy had created a pop-up image of himself with sketches of our time together. It was almost like a storyboard of our dates. It was the most remarkable thing I'd ever seen. He enclosed candid pictures of his rock-climbing and snowboarding, and some personal photos. He's truly a creative and artistic man. This gesture was far superior to anything a man had ever done for me before.

Months passed and we saw one another as often as possible. His time was limited, but we made it work. Our relationship was very new, and every time we got together, it was almost like we were getting to know one another all over again. This kept the relationship at more of a friendship level, and it just could not seem to make it any further. Ugh!

A year had passed, but we were still writing letters and saw one another any time we could. His career was taking off, and he began working for a prestigious magazine shooting big-time celebs like Michael Jordan.

Maybe it was the long distance aspect, or possibly the busy nature of our lives, but after time, we merely moved on.

Nearly ten years later, after filing for my divorce, we reconnected in Arizona. This was a story within itself! It involved George Clooney, Sammy Sosa, Michael Jordan, and a club called Axis and Radius! Thank goodness for witnesses, because no one would ever believe this one! Again, I'll save this for another time! This beautiful man had flown all the way to Scottsdale, and yet, we still could not find that connection that we had searched for.

Six years later, he visited Texas, and once again, we were in search of that connection. Finally, sixteen years later, Surfer Boy is no longer a boy. He moved into the big leagues and made the ultimate move.

It was a memorable, earth-shattering kiss. Yes, a mere kiss. Hey, I'll take what I can get at this point! Talk about taking your time to get to know one another. This potential love affair was the longest I had ever known. It had been the most mysterious and curious relationship of my life. It began innocently and always remained that way. Surfer Boy is now a well-renowned photographer and highly successful in his field. More importantly, he's successful in life. He's climbed the highest mountaintops, is an avid adventure thrill-seeker, and he's lived his life in joy. Over the years he's asked me to move to California and take that leap of faith, but I've never been able to do so. I've always considered myself to be the big risk-taker and thrill-seeker, but no one holds a candle to this man. In our relationship, he always put me first. He always came to me on my terms. Over the last seven years, I've wondered why I couldn't take that leap of faith. Well, I can't wait another seven years to find out, so my quest for love continues. I'm heading to California to find out once and for all; is he the one that got away? Stay tuned as the quest for true love continues.

Incredibly Tolerant

Dear Dating Diva:

How big a red flag is it that someone in a relationship is going through the other person's cell phone bills and e-mails and actually calling numbers to see if it's someone of the opposite sex? When there has never been any sign or hint of any issue or unfaithfulness in the relationship? Assuming this is just misplaced jealousy/control issues what do you do? Just say this isn't OK?

Dear Incredibly Tolerant:

Do you really need me on this one? You seem to be a fairly rational and tolerant individual. If you care for this person and want to work through this issue, talk to him/her! Sit him down in a neutral setting and have a calm, rational, and adult conversation. Try not to be confrontational, but rather ask discovery-type questions. Attempt to understand why. You'll learn so much about your partner during this time, and hopefully it'll only bring you closer. Your significant other is obviously insecure. Is it possible that someone cheated on him in a previous relationship? No matter, there is no excuse for this behavior. The manner that he chooses to engage in this conversation will speak volumes about his character and ability to have a healthy, loving, communicative, and trusting relationship. Also, I'd suggest that you define your boundaries, too. Going through someone's personal property is inappropriate behavior in any type of relationship, including good old-fashioned friendship. I wish you luck, and keep me posted on your outcome!

Frustrated and Disposable

Dear Dating Diva:

I'm frustrated with things that happen and don't happen when dating. I know that there are guys out there [who] can just simply show you that they care. I miss having someone [who] genuinely cares and worries about me. Someone [who] wants to make sure I get home safely—the little things [are] what mean the world to me. Why can't I find anyone like this? Do people actually care for one another any longer? Why are we so disposable to men?

Dear Frustrated & Disposable:

You are intimidating to men. You're spectacularly beautiful, sophisticated, well-travelled, articulate, educated, caring, and dress to the nines. You need a man who complements your beauty and inner strength, as do I! Boys cannot handle women like us. That's why they run from us. You deserve a *man*. A man is a rare, exquisite creature that should be nurtured once discovered. They are not myths! Keep holding your head up high and be on the lookout. Stop wasting your time with men who don't even open the door for you. They are not worth your time. As you said, the little things count, right?

Society dictates that we are to be amazing, career-oriented women, mothers, friends, sisters, and daughters. Wow, talk about a full-time job! Having accomplished all of the above, we deserve nothing less than the best, because that's what we give to others so freely. Allow yourself to attract a man who appreciates how priceless you are and that you have what it takes to be a woman!

Breakup Template Letter

After years of dating with long-term exposure to clueless men, I decided to create a breakup template letter, just for you! I believe, with minimal editing, it pretty much sums it up for most fabulous females. As Coty Cosmetics once advertised, "Make a statement without saying a word." In this case, just "Insert Name Here".

Warning: do not continue reading if you do not have a sense of humor!

Dear "Insert Name Here,"

We've been dating for a while and it's been great, but I have to tell you that I can't do this anymore.

I'm no longer interested in your empty promises, occasional sleepovers, late-night booty calls, drunken emotional texts, jealous rages, childlike exchanges, boy's nights, or failed attempts to make me jealous. Your actions have spoken louder than anything you could ever verbalize. You have behaved poorly in situations that called for decorum, been unresponsive to a 911 telephone call, and had a complete disregard for my well-being and feelings. I believed that you'd grow up at some point, but I was wrong. (See, I can say that I'm wrong!)

I'm not certain what your idea of dating or a relationship is, but where I come from, a man calls when he says he's going to, walks on the outside along a crowded sidewalk, opens a car door for a woman, tells her that she looks fabulous when it's apparent that she's put some effort into getting ready for an important dinner with you or has gone out of her way to plan a romantic evening.

You've much to learn about a real woman. She's confident, ambitious, loving, nurturing, sexual, and wants to have her cake and eat it too, all while wearing fierce five-inch stilettos. A real woman is not afraid of work, supporting her man in his endeavors, having a family, or making love to a man just because she feels like it. A real woman is in control of her sexuality and isn't afraid of letting go, but only when she's safe in the arms of a man who appreciates her for all that she is. For that matter, a real man anticipates the sexual arrival of the woman within and savors the moment. Only a real man has the capacity, class, intellect, depth, and open heart to allow a woman to discover herself while discovering him. An intense, explosive connection, both mentally and physically, comes when you freely give yourself to another. It's a shame that you've never allowed yourself to experience this with me or anyone else.

Truly, I wish you luck with your (*select all that apply*: bromance, job, drug habit, Star Wars memorabilia, or deviant nature collection), as it has become clear that this is the only relationship you'll ever be committed to.

As for me, it's time to try on the latest season's stilettos—I'm thinking cougar print. As they say, out with the old. Meow!

P.S. Please dispose of that DVD that we made; I wouldn't want it to fall into the wrong hands. You wish!

READER COMMENT FROM FACEBOOK:

Great template! Your description of a "real woman" is exciting and enticing. That paragraph alone would probably have him trying to come back for a second (or third or fourth) chance to show he can behave like a "real man."

PS, If I ever receive this letter from a woman, I'll be mighty upset with you (after I bitch slap myself for behaving this way, of course)!

"Truly, I wish you luck with your (*select all that apply*: bromance, job, drug habit, Star Wars memorabilia, or deviant nature collection)." Is it completely sad that I've dated guys who would check *all* of the above? I'm so glad to be out of the dating game. You are a brave woman!

Broken

Have you ever felt broken? Not broke, as we're all feeling that way these days! Truthfully, I question, is my quest for true love for naught? Am I naïve in longing for something that could be nonexistent in my personal realm? Will I ever find a love like I lost so many years ago? Is that love irreplaceable? Some say that there's only one true love for each of us—one soul mate. I pray that this isn't the case. Others have said, "Wait for it, and true love will find you." I emphatically disagree! I think that we must seek out true love and relish in the Quest as well as the pain. The quest for true love is what makes us appreciate and respect it once we've been captivated by it. The pain teaches us so much more. It teaches us what we will accept by way of compromise and what we will not tolerate. Hopefully it teaches us to be more understanding and kind to one another along the way. The only thing that could minimize the pain and constant aching is to embrace the idea of true love. We should welcome it into our lives no matter what obstacles we're facing. True love does conquer all! It can help us to get through the tough times and make the good times all that more exciting. I must have faith in this romantic notion! It cannot be a myth!

Personally speaking, is it possible that my idealistic views are the issue? Why do I say this? After much reflection, I think it's the fact that every man I've ever known leaves and fails to live up to the expectations he's committed to: loving his family, children, and wife. Maybe my expectations for support, love, honor, and appreciation are not realistic. From a generational standpoint, are we afraid of accepting love? Could it be due to broken homes, growing up as latchkey kids, cheating parents, alcoholism, or lack or religion in the home? Have any of the aforementioned issues imposed a sense of selfishness so that we can never give ourselves to another wholeheartedly?

I believe that our society has taught us to consistently trade up. That philosophy supports why most will not take a leap of faith—fear of being dumped and ultimately rejected! Being left alone, without a safety net and emotionally castrated, is not an appealing thought to any of us, right? I think the sense of being broken resonates from childhood experiences for most. If we acknowledge our personal patterns, we can break the cycle so that we no longer feel broken, and ultimately let love in. As always, I continue my passionate quest for true love with high expectations and savoring every second that I see a glimmer of hope.

READER COMMENT FROM FACEBOOK:

I believe there are many people with whom each of us can find true love. I believe good things do not come to those who wait, but to those who work for them. I believe in working to find true love and not settling for less (unless a child is involved, but there are exceptions to every rule). I believe even true love can fall apart if both partners do not work at it by spending a lifetime reminding one another through gentle sacrifices how much they mean to each other. I believe God loves us unconditionally and has gifted each of us with the capacity for true love so we may understand the love he has for us. I believe we are "broken" until we experience that gift. I believe I may be wrong in everything I believe, but choose to believe anyway.

I like your thought about a "trading up philosophy." Kind of like waiting on the bigger, better deal. Such a waste. We are a little broken. It is unavoidable just growing up and being socialized into adulthood. I absolutely agree that you have the right to expect of people that which they said they would do. Often, it seems to me that it's the unmet expectations of others that cause the most conflict.

What's Your Freak Flag?

Once upon a time, while having a fabulous girl's weekend in South Beach, I stumbled across an intriguing and most certainly non-ladylike conversation. Imagine six girls and two hotel rooms in the heart of party central. Already, you know it's going to be good story, right? It was a steamy evening at a posh restaurant, and the mojitos were steadily flowing. I don't know what it is about girls, but put us in a sexy dress and a pair of stilettos and suddenly we're invincible! I guess you'd feel that way too, if you could walk around on five-inch toothpicks all day! Anyway, this flirtatious, yet disturbing topic of conversation hit the table and our liquid courage kicked in. After my most recent encounter, inclusive of liquid courage, I must share the naughtiness with you!

Warning: This column is excessively graphic. In case of emergency, use the paper bag in the seat back pocket in front of you.

The topic: What's your freak flag?

Most freak flags should remain private, while sharing only with that special someone. Kind of like your secret fantasy list! (Yes, every girl has one, boys!) Whereas other freak flags should be kept to yourself. Really, please, my eyes are burning!

Freak Flag 1: What you do in the privacy of your bathroom should remain there. Let the throne be your own. Close the door, guys and dolls! Your beauty secrets and bonding moments should be kept private and confidential. Keep out!

Freak Flag 2: Golden showers. You're not Greek and we're not in Rome. Do I look like a fire hydrant?

Freak Flag 3: Funky spunk. Enough said!

Freak Flag 4: Ask and you shall receive? That depends on *where*. Hint: That's an innie, not an outtie.

Freak Flag 5: Pay close attention: a cow's heart, jumper cables, and electricity. Yes, I'm serious! Watch *1,000 Ways To Die* on

Spike TV. It is disturbing how much time people have on their hands.

Freak Flag 6: Pay attention, boys: ladies and lace, I repeat, ladies and lace. Nowhere in that statement did I say "men," correct? We do not, under any circumstances, want a visual of you wearing our black lace teddy. Resist the urge!

Freak Flag 7: Under the bed boxes. These are meant for sweaters, swimsuits, or other seasonal items. Not for human beings. Plus, we don't want to mess up our manicures!

Freak Flag 8: Alcohol should be consumed via your mouth. Ponder that thought, people!

Freak Flags 9 and 10: You've already thought of them for me!

My advice is direct in the case of freak flags. If you've seen any of your private flags on an episode of *Criminal Minds*, *Law and Order SVU*, or any other crime drama series, you might consider keeping it under wraps for good!

Believe it or not, after I really think about it, I have my own freak flag. Do you? Admit it, I bet you do!

READER COMMENT FROM FACEBOOK:

Classic! I can't believe you posted that, but I'm totally glad I read it. Any one of those freak flags could be worth an hour-long conversation. Throw them all into the mix, and that's a lot of laughs you ladies shared!

Number one is most likely to be forgotten after marriage and children. The little rats always seem to open the door at the most inappropriate time. After a while, it becomes more of a strong suggestion than a hard rule. I read about number eight somewhere several months back, and all I recall is that it's very dangerous—easy alcohol poisoning. As for number two, I've never actually known anyone who gets off from that behavior, or is at least willing to admit to it, thank God! That's one conversation I'd rather laugh about instead of share as a serious discussion. And number six, what's wrong? Scared the man will look better in it than the lady? Ha! He better not! Yeah, I have my own freak flags, and at least one of them is not on your list.

One

When I wake up I think of you
I close my eyes and dream of you
My heart is full, yet soon to break
As I can tell this is a mistake
You work too much
You neglect to call
This is why I'll never fall
For you do not value me
I pray that I begin to see
I guess it's time to get a clue
So now I shall say adieu
To not repeat my same mistake
As I control my ultimate fate
I've loved and lost, yet realize
The only cost is not a big surprise
Our time has passed
My heart does ache
I pray the lord has not decided my fate
To be alone and not to love
Would be like living without the sun
The air I breathe
The passion I feel
Is why my heart can be revealed
To only one.

READER COMMENT FROM FACEBOOK:

I really like the way this reads. I'm certain everyone can find a time or place in their lives where this has relevance and meaning. I know I felt as if it spoke to me. I just really liked how this read.

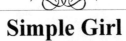

Simple Girl

I am a simple girl, not a superhero with an invisible cloak or a cape.

I am a simple girl who feels isolated, yet still confident in knowing who she is.

I am a simple girl who won't settle for anything less than what I know I am to be.

I am a simple girl who stands alone but hopes someone chooses to stand beside her.

I am a simple girl with simple tastes yet a refined sense of self.

I am a simple girl who is driven and determined, as I refuse to be a product of my environment.

I am a simple girl who enjoys baseball, riding a bike, and watching a scary movie, all while wearing my stilettos.

I am a simple girl who needs to feel safe; who longs to be touched by only one, and that's my Mr. Right.

I am a simple girl who loves my friends and cherishes those relationships, as they are my family.

I am a simple girl who, when compared to a book, reads like *Atlas Shrugged*.

I am a simple girl who wants everything yet needs nothing, except her true love.

I am a simple girl who has decided to embrace that superhero cape.

Here's to the quest for true love! May it take you to places near and far. May you find laughter along the way, and ultimately choose to be the superhero in your own Quest. Let nothing stand in your way!

The Huntress

There comes a time in every adult woman's life when she realizes it's time to take control and make things happen. About two years ago, I made that conscious decision to stop existing and commit to living!

I've always been the responsible one; the individual who makes good, solid, grounded decisions, but yet I have an adventurous side that fuels my independence. This is where I get into some serious trouble! Since I was a little girl, I knew that I'd travel to the pyramids and have an exciting life that others only dream of. I was never afraid to travel alone, dine solo, or go against the grain. Yet, my vantage point remains different than most. Personally, I view every day as an opportunity to be happy, to explore, to live, and to love. I believe in starring in my own life versus someone else's. I've thrived on not knowing what tomorrow brings. However, my "ready, fire, *then* aim" philosophy has left me where I am today—alone, independent, and still searching for someone similar to me. But now I find that wanting to change my existence in hopes of sharing my life with someone else was a foreign concept completely. How do I do this? How do I let go? How do I let someone else in? How do I allow someone else to make decisions on my behalf? (Yes, you guessed it. I'm a closet control freak!)

Consciously, I started to journal while keeping record of my relationships—the fabulous men I was so blessed to date—and begin to dissect what the challenges had been throughout our time together. (However, this is about me, not them!) I learned that I'm incredibly self-sufficient due to the fact that I've been completely on my own since I was seventeen years old. It's not that I want to be independent; it's that I've had no choice but to learn how to manage my life and recognize the consequence of poor choices. This independence has been a blessing and a curse in disguise. For example, it's OK to ask for help when opening a bottle of wine, allow a man to open a door for you, or simply order a dessert for you to share! Geez, I can be so dense sometimes! "Miss Independent"—can I drop kick her now? I can be such a diva sometimes!

I learned that all men are not created equal. They are all fabulous, but due to my vagabond background, I'm a bit more discriminating when looking for a mate. I need someone who is educated, diverse, and as adventurous as I am.

I learned that due to my travels and consistent moves as a child that I am far too trusting. I've always had to start over and begin a new life with each move. This has prompted me to be more candid when meeting new people. Naïvely, I expected others to share this quality. Unfortunately, I never considered that while I have my own motivations, so do others! This has been a frighteningly tough lesson. Think stalker!

I've learned not to give my heart so quickly and to wear a crash helmet when dating. Close your mouth and listen more than you talk. You'll learn more about the person you're dating versus the facade. There's no need to rush, and if you wait a little bit before rushing into intimacy, you might actually like the real person more than the mirror image they've shown you.

I've learned to allow myself to say what I want and what I need in order to be happy in a relationship. If someone truly cares for me and respects me, they're more willing to listen, discuss, and ultimately understand me. With this said, our relationship can progress and hopefully blossom into something that I merely write about today.

By analyzing my relationships, I've been able to create a more targeted, warrior-like approach in my quest for true love. I've become a highly skilled, well-equipped huntress, with expert marksmanship qualities, who will put a quiver down your spine, but only if you're my prey.

Signs

As time passes, I become increasingly numb to the little nuisances that each day brings. For instance, I had a dinner date scheduled for the evening and my date decided to call me at 7:00 PM to confirm. Now, it's not that I'm not irritated by the lack of courtesy or respect for my time. It's merely that I would have to care enough to let it ruin my day. As time passes, I realize that one's bad manners, extraordinary lack of decorum, and basic common sense do not get under my skin as they did when I was twenty-one. Today, I value good manners, honesty, candor, friendship, as well as considerate communication. So to answer the question on everyone's minds, no, I did not go to dinner with this "speed bump" of a man. Quite frankly, why would I allow myself to be an afterthought in anyone's day? This person has clearly put out an Amber Alert to his behavior, right? Can you see where I'm going with this? Isn't it obvious? It's all about signs!

SIGN DECODER:

Deer Crossing: You're about to get bucked!

Falling Rocks: Historical data shows that he's a heartbreaker but well worth the fall and ultimate devastation.

Slippery Road Ahead: Slow down, be cautious, and it'll be worth the wait!

School Zone: You both have much to learn about relationships and a lot of growing up to do. So why not do it together?

Sharp Curve Ahead: You're about to experience something significant in your relationship. The manners in which you address the issue and communicate with one another will determine if your relationship crashes and burns!

When dating, it's not about what someone says to you, but rather what they do. Its cliché, yes, but actions do speak louder than words. Actions are signs! When dating, don't just glance at the signs. Read them! Yes, some signs are in braille and others are like freaking smoke signals. Nevertheless, the signs are visible. Stop, look, and respect them. In turn, you've respected yourself.

My Serendipitous Someone

Sometimes life just happens, and then there's something called serendipity. Some believe serendipity to be a moment of chance or opportunity, much like seeing a shooting star for the first time. I believe that life is magical. I believe that every person who we encounter is a beautiful constellation of surprise and wonder. We need merely to study, admire, and bask in the illumination of each. Every encounter can be as complex or as simplistic as you choose to make it. Although difficult at times, I choose to appreciate the beauty that lies within each encounter.

I was at a genuinely chaotic point in my life. It was a time where anything that could go wrong, was in fact, going wrong. It was a time when I genuinely needed a good friend and a safe place to rest my head. My closest girlfriends had been nothing but supportive, concerned, and loyal. I felt like everything was out of control, and that I was on the brink of losing everything. I am the girl who has always led a charmed life! With ease, I've always gotten what I needed and wanted, with the exception of true love. What's so ironic is that this is when I met my serendipitous someone. This encounter is one that I will always revel in as there were numerous road blocks in our way. For instance, three non-related friends had tried to introduce us, while three others told us not to meet. My motto has always been judge people based on how they treat you. With that concept in mind, I decided to take a chance and meet this mystery man. Going through all that I had been, I wasn't in a position to get into a serious relationship or become involved in an intimate manner. So I convinced myself, *what the heck—we can be friends*. Over many months, this serendipitous someone proved himself to be patient, kind, generous, attentive, and most importantly, my friend.

Initially, the time we spent together was disconnected. We were in the "getting to know you" phase, and our time together was infrequent. After the first date, I recall telling one girlfriend that he wasn't my type. However, something told me to go out with him again … and again. He was understated, sincere, fascinating, a dedicated father, well-educated, and in certain moments of greatness, possessed a wicked sense of humor. Yet during our first few dates, I still didn't feel that magnetic chemistry most of us believe to be a deal breaker. However, with my keen Dating Diva senses on high alert, I knew that this man was very special, and no matter what happened next, he'd be in my life forever.

As the months passed, our friendship blossomed, but life as we knew it consumed us. It was difficult to admit, but the truth was evident. Shooting stars eventually fizzle out, as did our passion and commitment to getting to know one another. The level of thoughtfulness and intimacy declined, not by choice, but rather by design. We were destined to be friends and nothing more. Dinner dates turned into pizza with the kids. Phone calls turned into a hassle versus a thrill. I began to feel like an afterthought and rather like someone who was being neglected, like when your significant someone gives you a candle for your birthday versus a love letter with flower petals. I would call that a sign, wouldn't you? Again, an afterthought. Ouch, talk about the truth hurting!

As many of you know, I'm looking for spectacular. I'm looking for that one moment of bliss that when found, I'll never let it go. I'm in search of that magical constellation of stars that has yet to be discovered and explored. I'm looking for warmth, honesty, care, concern, and someone who is loyal. It's an instant bond or connection that is visibly electric and radiant. It's much like how you feel when you're in New York.

Although this Dating Diva adventure didn't end in true love, it doesn't mean that I cannot appreciate it. The magical gift that remains is that two people can appreciate one another, be attracted to one another, and yet ultimately are not meant to be. With mutual respect and admiration, it just makes it harder to call it quits sometimes. It's not that anyone did anything wrong (unless you consider the candle), or that something could've been done differently. Sometimes friendship is all that remains. That's why I consider him "my serendipitous someone." He will always be my special gift, my special someone that with great fortune, was discovered and explored. Thank goodness for gift receipts, though!

READER COMMENT FROM FACEBOOK:

Ah, serendipity! One of my favorite words of the English language! While the word itself is defined by an "accidental fortuitous discovery," because without such a discovery the word would never be used, it also represents an aptitude for making such discoveries. It is therefore a word that exudes positivity in the present and future sense. In other words, although it was serendipity for you to meet that man, I sense from your writings that your active life is filled with serendipitous encounters. I wish you continued luck and hope that your serendipitous search ends with just one more moment of serendipity.

He wasn't the guy for you from the first moment. It's good you never give up. The right one might just be on the left side of you. I hope you get what that means. Sometimes when you are looking up for something, it was right down in front of you. You are one of kind. Peace to you.

A Novice Guide to Fishing—For a Man

When I was a little girl growing up in Pascagoula, Mississippi, some of my fondest times were spent fishing with my father and my brother, Todd. We'd take the boat out and anchor under an old bridge, or head to Dauphin Island and troll the weekends away.

Besides learning how to select the proper weight and lure, bait my own hook, cast off, and scale my own fish, I learned many lessons without even knowing it. Parents are sneaky sometimes, aren't they? One lesson specifically that comes to mind is that my father would say, "Little Bit, there are many different types of fish in the sea, but a proper fisherman only keeps the best. The ones that aren't quite grown—just throw them back. I'm sure they'll do for someone else." It's amazing after all these years that my father's words still remain so vivid. Most importantly, the advice he shared is incredibly relevant!

Now, we've all heard the expression about there being many different types of fish in the sea, right? Well here's how it relates to dating! So grab your CCA card (www.ccatexas.org) and follow along, for this is "A Novice Guide to Fishing—For a Man!"

Catfish—Run of the mill, bottom-feeder that'll consume just about anything. Catfish are typically located in old, creepy surroundings with little to no light, like your corner neighborhood pub or after-hours bar. The slimier, the better! Typically, catfish linger in outer areas in order to remain in stealth mode. Do not let this mode deceive you. They want to be caught and only "prey" that they are not released. Catfish are best when heavily battered in beer!

Sea Bass—Tend to have large mouths, thick heads, and are rather flaky. Sea bass can sometimes be fatty, with little nourishment to your soul. Sea bass inhabit near-shore areas. They don't like to leave their natural surroundings and travel in packs. Sea bass are located in high-impact areas with lots of light and reflection, such as your local muscle-head gym with full-length mirrors. They are beautiful to admire and appreciate. Remember to pose then flex, as this will ensure your ultimate heavyweight catch.

Shark—The most dangerous; a true predator—difficult to catch and can only be appreciated when fully contained, or dead. Sharks are located just about everywhere. Go swim, fish, and dine at Mo's Steakhouse with extreme caution. It's better to have all of your body parts, including your soul, intact than to attempt to wrangle in one of these predators! Warning: no chumming the waters! Safety advisory: all regulatory equipment and protective gear must be worn, including your rubber suit. You never know where these beasts will bite!

Tuna—The most common of the fish species and most suitable anytime or anyplace. Tuna can be found in a pouch, in a can, freshly sliced on a bed of rice, or grilled with a touch of balsamic vinegar. It's common and easily attainable as it's not overly pricey. Tuna is everywhere. The catch is that is must be fresh. If not, you're in for some rough nights ahead. Tuna can be found at any sports bar, golf course, or any art deco sushi shack east of the Mississippi. For the record, there's nothing wrong with tuna!

Blue Marlin—For a more sophisticated palate and those who desire something that is majestic and beautiful to admire. The blue marlin is an effort to catch, yet worth the cuts and scrapes one endures while getting it aboard. The blue marlin is strong, elusive, wild, and independent, and can rage through the water—and air—in order to evade capture. The blue marlin can be found where only the truest of fisherman is willing to venture. The blue marlin is elegant, luminescent, and the most beautiful of all. Blue marlin is best discovered through patience, forethought, and precise targeting with specialized bait and wide nets!

The most important lesson I trust you'll retain from "A Novice Guide to Fishing—For a Man" is that if you continue fishing under that creepy, old bridge, you're still going to end up with catfish! I don't know about you, but I'm looking for deeper waters, the bluest of skies, and the grandest catch of them all, because, have you seen what a blue marlin can do with its dorsal fin?

So keep the Cliffs notes. My work here is done, and I'm going fishing!

*Dedicated to Nicole, who inspires my quest for true love with her wisdom, good humor, and dedication to the truth and not The Fish Tale!

Closure

I'm one of the rare women who can maintain friendships with men that I've dated. However, I believe that it has to do with my superhuman ability to turn off my emotions, much like a light switch. This is not necessarily a good trait! While writing about my quest for true love, I've had several historical figures (a.k.a. exes) approach me to explain why things didn't work out. Gents, this is a question that all women desperately crave the answer to. As you well know, we overanalyze every little detail in our relationships. Closure allows us to move on. So take note! As I've stated numerous times, some couples, no matter how perfect they are for one another, just don't work out. Maybe it has to do with timing, the fact that they are too much alike, or that life just got in the way. For whatever reason, one specific historical figure had the fortitude and respect for our friendship to step up and provide what I needed—closure.

It was a random encounter at the neighborhood Starbucks. It had been nearly six months since last I saw him. I ordered my usual iced venti chai latte, as did he. We began what most could see was an uncomfortable greeting. You know, the typical, "Hi! How are you? How's life? What's new?" Most would deem this to be a fifth-grade level of conversation. However, it couldn't be further from the truth. As he drew a blank and the expressions on his face disturbingly began to change, I knew this was going to be a bombshell. He asked if I'd sit and chat with him for a bit. I agreed. He said he needed to tell me something. Wow, my curious nature was getting the best of me. Initially, I thought he was looking for absolution, or a way back into my life. Let's just say my thoughts were a little premature. As we sipped our drinks, he attempted to speak. The words were far from easy to formulate. I could see his hands trembling as his lips began to move. He proceeded to tell me that while we were dating, he had cheated on me. As it turned out, she got pregnant. He said that he was too ashamed to tell me before. He'd hoped that somehow I could forgive him. He wanted me to understand why things ended as abruptly as they did. To my own amazement, I felt like a weight had been lifted. I'd thought all along, it *was* him and not me. Ah, validation, and yet shamefully, this was a relief to me. Although his life has changed, he ultimately found peace in his decision. For that, I am happy. Yet, he lives with the result of his random, alcohol-induced, late night decision. As for me, I understood why and forgave him. Today, I can appreciate how when a man says, "I just can't explain it to you, you wouldn't understand," that quite possibly, he might be dealing with something far greater than I can fathom. My point is that at times it really isn't about us! Sometimes life happens and you end up not starring in your own Lifetime movie of the week.

READER COMMENT FROM FACEBOOK:

I applaud you for the strength to be able to push your feelings aside. Unfortunately, I know all too well the pain of forced closure, but closure is closure right? All we can do is learn from those relationships which have been thrown to the wind and forgotten. Once again, bravo and kudos on the strength. We all have it in us, but very few use it.

Want Ad

When I initially started working on *Dating Diva Adventures*, I viewed it no differently than having an introductory business meeting. What I realized is that in business, you strive to know as much about the prospect that you're meeting with as you can. It's all about gathering intelligence and information, right? The intended outcome is that you find synergy and conclude that there is a reason to have continued discussions, correct?

Another vantage point to consider is that when seeking employment, you view job postings which have detailed requirements about the position. Then, mentally you create a relational spreadsheet that allows you to determine if you're qualified or not. Again, gathering information!

These vantage points made me think, why not look at my personal wants/needs/desires in the same manner? Much like all of the successful dating sites like Match.com, E-Harmony and Setformarriage.com have done. It's a concept that I was certainly slow to catch on to, duh!

So with some diligent thought, I proceeded to create and maintain my own personal want ad!

Keep in mind; it only takes one candidate—kind of like hitting the lottery!

Personal Want Ad

Five-foot, seven-inch blonde, blue-eyed, slender, professional, goofy, adventurous, fun, sophisticated female seeks grounded, rational, considerate, witty, educated, well-travelled man with a lust for life and a dedication to family and friends.

Position Requirements:

-    Must be a kind-natured person; good manners are essential

- Must be an articulate communicator; written, verbal, or smoke signals—just make the effort

- Must have, or aspire to have, a toned physique

- Must be 6'1" or above

- Must have eyes that speak volumes and have a twinkle that keeps me longing for more

- Must be able to assimilate into different environments—jeans to a tux

- Must enjoy the outdoors—golf, baseball, running, cycling, swimming, soccer, skiing, etc.

- Must be goal-oriented; a man with a plan

- Must be spontaneous at times

- Must be a "believer"

- Must have passion and possess conviction—*not* a conviction

- Must possess a wicked sense of humor or have the ability to find humor in each day

- Must be able to lounge on the sofa and watch a movie or enjoy a night on the town if so desired

- Must be able to enjoy the arts—fine art, books, museums, architecture, and all varieties of music

- Must be able to grab a bite at Beck's Prime as easily as Fleming's

- Must be able to effortlessly let me know I'm cared for with his actions rather than purchases—for example, a handwritten note of affection or a genuine compliment about the not-so-obvious

- Must be able to lead and/or participate in a good verbal banter

- Must smile as often as possible; no posers

- Must be able to receive and give affection; intimacy at all levels is a necessity

- Understands the art of kissing and how it affects women on an emotional and physical level

- Enjoys sex and is willing to explore all the possibilities

- Must be able to speak the truth; sometimes it may hurt but, it is what it is

- Must have good hygiene; man-scaping is optional— maintained is preferred

- Must be able to appreciate and respect the individual who possesses the above mentioned requirements

Compensation Package:

I have only my heart and unconditional love to offer, but will commit to being a friend, partner, and the one who loves you more than life itself. My desire is to let you (us) dream and for us to share in the risk while pursuing those dreams.

Disclaimers:

* No married man need apply or respond to this ad

* No separated man need apply or respond to this ad

* No man that has a current girlfriend or is living with his ex-girlfriend need apply or respond to this ad

READER COMMENT FROM FACEBOOK:

"Living with his ex-girlfriend," classic! "What? Oh her! Listen, I've been meaning to tell you about that. You see, it's like this ..." followed by complete BS. However, my favorite is the part where your man can have passion and conviction, but not "a conviction." But what if he has a conviction based on passion—a passionate conviction, so to speak? What? Hell no? You're a hard woman to please.

The Economics of Dating

While dining with friends and enjoying a fabulous bottle of Pinot Noir, we began discussing our work, upcoming travels, Obama in the classrooms, and, you guessed it, dating. This wasn't the typical dating conversation, though. This involved more of the economics of dating.

The conversation quickly turned heated as both sexes defended their positions and expenses as they relate to a night on the town with the opposite sex. Frankly, I'd never really considered how expensive it is for one date, let alone multiple dates during one week. We each gained a greater respect and appreciation for the almighty dollar!

Ladies, do you realize how truly expensive it is for men these days? Think about it! Dinner with drinks can be $150.00 without dessert. Add a movie to the night, and you could be looking at $210.00 for one night out!

Men, do you realize how expensive it is for women? Contrary to popular belief, we don't wake up looking fabulous. It takes a little grooming. Frankly, you don't want us showing up with jacked-up nails, a unibrow, or a mustache, do you? On average, women could pay $20.00 for a manicure, $35.00 for a pedicure, $25.00 for waxing, and $40.00 for hair. What if we decided to purchase a new blouse for the big date? Add $50.00. That gives us a total of around $55.00-$170.00. This scenario doesn't even account for childcare. Wow!

Bottom line, dating is expensive for both men and women.

My advice is stop wasting your hard-earned money on guys/girls that you're merely giving a chance to.. In the "getting to know you phase," let's be respectful and consider going for coffee, going to Discovery Green, or going for a walk in the park. Once you get to know someone, and if they're truly interested in you, then and only then can you decide what the economics of dating are worth to you!

READER COMMENT FROM FACEBOOK:

Are you claiming that most women get a $20 manicure, $35 pedicure, $25 waxing, $40 hairdo, and buy a $100 outfit, for that total of $220, every time they go on a first date? Good lord, keep such a narcissistic (not to mention ridiculously high-maintenance) woman away from me! If she's not self-assured enough to feel like she can impress me with her personality and who she is as a person, rather than primarily with her artificially (and temporarily) enhanced appearance, she's not [my] kind of woman! Give me real!

This is an excellent point on both ends. Folks need to get creative on how to get to know each other. It does not take [money] to know someone and truly value the best parts. All it takes is the basics; getting back to the natural state.

I hate to say it, but you forgot to amortize the cost of your Louis Vuitton handbags and your Jimmy Choos. You make a good point: the economics of dating are probably a lot more equitable than we men ever imagined—and out of control.

My Life

In recent months, it's become apparent that while sharing my life and dating experiences in such an open forum, it's leaving little for me at the end of each day, and it's putting others needlessly on display. It's become apparent that my life and my choices have been inadvertently open for interpretation, speculation, and at times, degradation. For clarification, it's my life and I'm proud to say that:

My life has great adventure and has always been full of surprise.

My life is filled with spontaneous moments, some of which I can never speak.

My life is exciting and has never-ending promise.

My life is yet to come full circle.

My life is not what I had planned, and yet I am thankful.

My life doesn't have a great love but is filled with the greatest of love.

My life has only one regret.

My life is mine and only I can make decisions for me.

My life is challenging, but that's what keeps me strong and determined and provides clarity each day.

My life is a contradiction from an outsider's point of view.

My life is like an artist's canvas that is awaiting its next colorful brushstroke.

My life is filled with joy thanks to the company I keep, the choices I make, and the way I choose to approach each day.

My life is worth living, and I choose to live it out loud.

My life is worth seeking out great love and I choose to embrace the journey.

My life deserves to be shared with someone who is worthy of me.

Doesn't yours?

READER COMMENTS FROM FACEBOOK:

Apparently, you have received some negative feedback about the inclusion of this line in your recent column: "My life deserves to be shared with someone who is worthy of me." Interestingly enough, this is something I have been thinking a lot about lately and I tend to agree with you. I am a huge people-watcher and like to observe other people and their interactions with each other, and lately I have noticed a lot of married people [who] don't look happy. It has made me ask myself if that is what marriage is about—a total compromise of happiness to be married. Anyway, despite the feedback you have received from others, I applaud you for living your life the way you do and trying to find someone that is right for you. At the very least, you are trying and not compromising and selling yourself short.

I forget if I read this in one of your columns, but have you been married before? I think that people [who] have been married once before see things somewhat differently than people who have never been married. We kind of know what it is that we are looking for this time around. And for those of us [who] respect and believe in the sanctity of marriage, we want to get it right, because we don't want to be one of those people [who] marry three, four, five, or even more times.

Embrace imperfection. I am someone [who] has been married and divorced. I even married one man twice. Let me share with you that while I was young and flighty (I refuse to say stupid), I felt that "exciting" was the way to roll. It was. I had a very colorful life. I still do. The difference today is, however, that with wisdom and total clarity, I can reflect on my life with wiser eyes. I say marry your best friend. That old adage about how important it is to grow old with someone [who] makes you laugh and you can really talk with is most important! I think there are many great guys, sexy guys, funny guys, intelligent guys, but a man [who] will make you laugh and loves living is divine. I have a husband [who] is so wonderful. He is a Christian; he is tall and lanky and has a lovely smile and beautiful blue eyes. He loves people and children. I adore him. Last, but certainly not least, my best advice is to marry someone that loves God and understands the meaning of life here and in the hereafter.

I don't embrace imperfection, but I do accept it as being part of life in the imperfect world that we all live in. Once I accepted the fact that there is no perfect woman to aspire to be with, my life became much happier and easier. Then it became more a matter of focusing on my own self and working at being the best man I could be to be able to offer someone something of value—myself, as a truly good man who is a giver, not a taker. If it's not a mutual win/win, it won't work.

I love the way you put things. You seem to have a great heart. I like the canvas thing you say. I want to be inside your head more. I will read more of your writings, which I think [are] great. Keep the words coming and I will keep on reading.

Sorry to hear about your bad luck in the fidelity department. My personal opinion of people who cheat is that they should be hung upside down by their toes and left to twist slowly in the wind. Nothing upsets me more than to hear of a man cheating on a good woman. There is no excuse in life for that! I'm sorry, but I get emotional about that issue. Most of my better friends are women; I would shoot the SOB that did that to one of my friends!

In the Crossroads

Notice This isn't your typical *Dating Diva Adventure* article, as nothing about the events on this day are frivolous.

Like most of us in America, I think about job stability, world affairs, health, finances, and long-term security. I've just opted not to include such serious topics in my column. We'll leave that to the news! Instead, I've kept it lighthearted and playful. Yesterday, I realized that for every problem that's been weighing on me, it was minute in comparison to what I experienced in a crossroad.

It was a typical work day and I was hustling from one meeting to the next. I had a couple of conference calls and two client meetings under my belt by 2:50 PM. I looked tired, yet fortunately had time to quickly freshen up before hosting a cocktail party downtown, at The Lancaster Hotel. As I drove on Richmond heading toward downtown, I could feel myself becoming impatient as I caught the red light at Hazard. I was in the far left lane and preparing to turn. As I awaited the light, a black Chevy Silverado pickup truck came through the light in order to make a left-hand turn onto Richmond. At that very moment, I witnessed something that I would never wish upon another human being. As the driver made his turn, with much force, he struck not one, but two small children as they followed behind their mother in the crosswalk, much like ducklings. I could see the mother's hand as it released the daughter's hand and she was swept under the truck. The little girl was underneath the truck; face down on the hot asphalt. She lay helpless and still. The little boy in his red shirt and khaki pants lay crumbled on the concrete pavement, nonresponsive.

The sound of them being struck is deafening and peculiar; much like the sound if you run over an empty cardboard box. Without hesitation, all of us who witnessed the pink Hello Kitty backpack take flight were in tears. The mother screamed in agony and disbelief. The driver stopped. He was perplexed and searching for what he had struck. Finally he saw. He was shocked as he discovered one child, but then purely disgusted with himself as he saw the second. He raised his hands and clasped his head in despair. He was visibly devastated. His voice shrieked with pain. He was visibly shaken and I could only assume heartbroken. The father ran out of the convenient store with rage as witnesses stopped him from doing anything he should not. A man jumped from his car and ran up to the black Silverado and crawled partially under the truck in order to potentially calm the little girl. At first, there was just silence; no tears, no movement, and no honking horns, even as traffic began to back up. Everyone felt an enormous sense of disbelief and sorrow as they stood helpless in the crossroads.

Without haste, fire rescue arrived on the scene. Suddenly, I heard the faint sounds of the children crying over the sounds of the fire trucks. The two small children were delicately placed onto one gurney, so that they could comfort one another.

I can only say that the sorrow I felt for this family is something that I had never experienced before. Although I have experienced great loss, I have never experienced the potential loss of a child.

I hope to discover the condition of these two small souls and will pray that at some point I understand what greater plan is involved in this senseless event. For, at a crossroads, two small lives were changed, along with every person who was witness.

The love that I so desperately search for is no match for this, my dear reader. The love of a child and potential loss of a child, including their innocence, is the greatest love on earth. I am embarrassed at the selfish life I lead, humbled, and feel incredibly foolish as I worry about myself and the petty problems I face.

Know that writing helps me to cope. It is how I express myself; a way to heal and urge others to pay attention when driving. It's the little things that mean the most, especially in the crossroads.

READER COMMENTS FROM FACEBOOK:

What an emotional read and quite the awakening. Thank you for sharing what must have been a difficult experience for you. Try and update us on the two small souls if you find out their condition.

I'm sorry to hear that. We have clients that come to us for help after their child is killed in an accident. Although we are there to get them compensation for their loss, it is painful for me as I hear the story about their loss. I'll say a prayer for you.

Your story reminds us of how precious and fleeting life can be. Thank you for sharing. I say this as I get up to go kiss both of my boys to tell them how much I love them.

Thank you for the message in this story. It brings such an awakening. Sorry for the little angels, but it also is a gift from them to us. We need to learn from their story. Thank you for writing it!

Excellent job in writing this, as usual. And thank you for sharing your story. But, I'm sorry for what caused the story to be written. It does remind us that things like this happen all the time; we just don't see or hear about them a lot. Life-changing experiences of that nature can affect people who are part of them for reasons independent of each other. Fate can be part of the mix. It may have been meant for you to witness that for your own change of perspective on life.

Love

My love life is like most but unlike any other. For true love is what I covet, yet it has escaped me—much like the black crocodile Birkin! It's a topic that I discuss openly, and I have no regrets for my candor. For my words and yours have given me strength to continue my journey. For those who know me appreciate that I live for the unexpected and thrive on risk. I welcome the unknown but am crushed once my journey ends. It's the realization that what I've searched for and believe to have discovered is merely a mirage that saddens me. For the quest for true love is my Achilles heel. It has taken me to places near and far.

However, through my amazing adventures, I've come to understand that there are many different types of love.

Puppy Love—This is the most innocent, memorable, and purest of all forms of love. Remember those magical words handed to you on a piece of white-lined paper: do you love me? Circle Yes or No.

First Love—It's all about firsts—first kiss, first dance, first date, first sexual encounter … first pregnancy test!

Romantic Love—Boy chases girl. Girl crushes on boy. Boy courts girl and asks for her hand in marriage. They live happily ever after—plus one.

Power Love—Women have a tendency to fall for men who are in powerful positions. We find power tres sexy. Women salivate over strong, well-spoken, and educated men. This one isn't a shocker! Think Donald and Melania Trump.

Security Love—He makes you feel safe. You never have to worry. He takes care of everything. You might not have that physical passion that you've had in other relationships, but you'll sacrifice it for safety. Belvedere Vodka and Tylenol, anyone?

Daddy Love—You admire and respect him. He teaches you about life and molds you into a better version of yourself. Eventually you grow up and become your own person. Everyone knows what happens when you grow up, right? It's time to move on and spread your wings.

Passionate Love—The sexual chemistry is smoldering and is infinite. Your body pulsates as your mind races out of control with thoughts of your next physical encounter. No conversation necessary. Commitment is not mandatory, but discretion is. You will give up everything for this relationship. It is liberating, yet highly destructive, as eventually you'll want more than the other person can offer you.

Toxic Love—Love that resides in chaos, distrust, and constant fighting. You cannot seem to break the ties that bind you to this individual as this type of relationship is all you've ever known. In your mind this is normal. It is the only type of love you've ever personally experienced or witnessed. Healthy love is within your grasp if you deem yourself worthy of accepting it into your life. Toxic love must be disposed of as it will contaminate all the other aspects of your life. Take out the trash, people!

Virtual Love—The most dangerous love of all as your mind is very powerful. In virtual love, your imagination takes over and the fantasy begins. You meet online and begin what may seem as an innocent friendship. You share your life, likes/dislikes, deepest fantasies, and desires, while never sharing in the reality of everyday life. In your mind, you create a romanticized image of the perfect person —a person who you truly do not know, other than through e-mail exchanges. The ability to speak freely and become whomever you wish is freeing, and your mind is overpowered by your heart. Your heart is no longer yours, and yet you don't know who it belongs to, either! This is an episode of *Dateline* waiting to happen!

True Love—This is effortlessly giving in and bearing your soul to another. True love is sharing your deepest desires and loving someone more than you love yourself, all while knowing that rejection is possible. In this rare form of love, you become a better person. It happens when you least expect it, when you most need it, and when your heart is open to it.

Like I said, there are many different types of love, many of which may be right for you. Just realize that love isn't perfect and it isn't safe. Love is unconditional and selfless. Love can be overwhelmingly beautiful and is the most magical gift you can ever give. Love is worth the journey no matter where it takes you! So grab your passport and Chanel carry-on. Spain, anyone?

READER COMMENTS FROM FACEBOOK:

During your quest, you undoubtedly have had fun. True love comes from our Lord's placement within us! You, of course, already know this. Love to you, my long-time friend.

I love seeing what smart, talented women have to say on this subject. It's so fascinating from the male perspective to see what women who are seemingly obsessed with the whole subject of love— or more specifically, true love—say about it. It's a smart man who can read between the lines to see inside the psyche of such women. It teaches us a lot about the inner person. We might not always read it correctly, but it sure does help in understanding the person's life motivations!

Your Letters Addressed

The Million Dollar Question is: why are you single?

By choice! My *Dating Diva Adventures* book isn't about couple-dom, nor is it about marriage. It's about true love and the journey in finding yourself along the way. What have you learned about yourself? What do you lack? What do you need versus want? What can't you live without? I'm looking for true love, not companionship or a free meal. I do not wish to just tolerate another human being. I do not date losers or those without goals and high expectations of themselves. Would you?

I treat people with respect and kindness and show gratitude each day. It's that whole "do unto others" concept. I guess it kind of stuck with me as a child. I'm looking for someone with a zest for life and adventure. I love risk and appreciate the unexpected! I want someone who makes me smile each day by being himself. However, he's got to physically excite me, too! Chemistry is mandatory!

I'm not looking for the game-player who may text me three words and I text three words back. If you're interested, show it! I have no energy for stupid human tricks! Now, this may sound a little self-important, but I believe that I'm somewhat misunderstood as my exterior is a contradiction to my interior. Almost like *Pimp My Ride*. Deep down, I'm still the nice, yet plain girl who was a bookworm in school. I was popular but not the most popular. Make sense? I've worked hard for everything and seized the opportunities in front of me. Growing up in a double-wide, you kind of have to! Nothing has been handed to me and I don't expect it to be. I choose to be nice every day. I choose to be polite and I choose to be single because I'm looking for that one person who can be honest, kind-natured, and make me feel like the most beautiful girl in the room, even with my Yankees cap and Converse on! I'm not the doll in the dress twenty-four-seven. Most girls aren't. I am multifaceted, intelligent, strong, yet naïve at times. I am grateful for every sunset I can view and make it a point to find laughter in my day everyday! Most times, I'm laughing at myself. I enjoy time with my girlfriends and appreciate nothing more than going crazy on a dance floor.. I am not a toy. I am not an object. I have feelings and want to be treated with respect, all while giving the same respect to my love interest. If any of this makes sense, then and only then will you understand why I am single!

For now, I will remain single and will not date again until I find that special someone. Or maybe he will find me. This "show" is over. I'm exhausted! However, the column continues as does the final chapter of the book, with my dating advice and insane escapades. Stay tuned, as this ride's not over! Virtual dating, anyone?

READER COMMENTS FROM FACEBOOK:

I enjoyed it again. Your reasons for being single are similar to mine, except I won't be wearing a Yankees cap anytime soon. I believe I told you before that I am wrapping up my book on the adventures in adult dating—man there is lot of space in that subject. Knowing when to stop writing (or bringing up new topics on the matter) can be the most daunting part, but it was the same for my parenting book. I finally just said enough, and the rest goes in the sequel. Have fun with your stuff. I am surely enjoying my adventure.

Yes, that was the million dollar question.

I came across a line from Henry Miller (about his own writing) that I thought you will enjoy: "Whatever I do is done out of sheer joy; I drop my fruits like a ripe tree. What the general reader or the critic makes of them is not my concern."

Keep writing. Keep following your passions. It is such a pleasure to watch because it is unfortunately such a rare event that someone does just that.

A Woman

To see your face,
Then your smile,
That's when my body becomes aroused.

I have no choice,
It's human nature,
My mind is numb,
My hands are shakier.

My thighs quiver as I await,
It's overwhelming, make no mistake.

He captivates,
As he takes hold,
My body aches,
My body knows,

I give myself willingly,
As I know that he can set me free.

For this release is the epitome of everything I can truly be,
A woman.

Virtual Soul Mate

WARNING: EXTREME DANGER
What you're about to read is not realistic nor rational.
Please back away slowly and proceed with caution!

Out of the blue,
Into my life,
To mesmerize and enchant.

Your words are extreme,
Somehow it seems,
This makes perfect sense.

You've entered my life,
Touched my heart,
Elevated my sight.

You know my name,
I know your game,
Where's my common sense?

For that I have lost,
Or rather tossed aside,
As my head no longer takes the lead.

With a shiver down my spine,
I know it is time,
For this love to take flight.

Will Italy bring many splendid things?
Could this be the final chapter?

For that is unknown,
Yet let it be told,
My destiny waits,
My virtual soul mate.

Dating Diva—Valentine's Day—Top Ten

Hallmark holidays appeal to many people, but as for me, I'm not a huge fan. They remind me of "T-shirt fans"—those who wear logo gear during a playoff game but cannot tell you a thing about a team's season. Understand? I much prefer acts of kindness or tokens of one's affection to be shown when they feel the urge and not because some marketing or PR firm tells them to do so. However, Valentine's Day is just around the corner and your e-mails are demanding. *What do I get my girlfriend for Valentine's Day?* Guys, this is so incredibly simple that I cannot believe I'm even going to spell-check this article! Keep it simple, silly! Women merely want to know that we're cared for, loved, appreciated, or that you think we're beautiful and sexy! So here's my top ten list of ideas just for you!

1. Write her a note telling her how you feel or what makes her special to you. (She has a kind heart, her hair smells like cotton candy, her eyes twinkle like the lights that illuminate the skyline, or her smile makes you forget all of your worries.)

2. Go to the florist and buy a bag of rose petals and sprinkle them where appropriate. Let your imagination be your guide.

3. Make a CD of your favorite music and give it to her. This makes her feel closer to you. No joke!

4. Purchase a bottle of champagne and listen to your CD together! We want to be alone with you—music and champagne—your night is headed in the right direction for sure!

5. Take her bowling, sailing, kayaking, or skeet shooting. Activities bond couples. Do things that make you laugh! Honestly, going to dinner gets boring after awhile, right?

6.   If you must purchase jewelry, nothing says elegance and taste like the timeless Tiffany's blue box. Tiffany's has something for every price range, too. Don't be shy! "Nothing bad ever happens at Tiffany's." (Wink, wink to Audrey Hepburn.)

7.   I've noticed that the art of romance is nonexistent these days. Let me remind you of slow dancing. This one is so easy! Turn up the music and turn down the lights; hold her close and dance with her. When was the last time you slow danced? Remember how good it felt?

8.   If you're more traditional, take her to dinner with candlelight, champagne, chocolate-covered strawberries, and dancing. You merely need to bring your wallet, boys!

9.   From "I like you," to "I love you," to "I cannot live without you," it's Valobra, baby! You'll find diamonds, emeralds, rubies, sapphires, and custom creations like no other. Tell Franco that I sent you.

10.   Ladies love luxurious lingerie! La Mode Lingerie on West Gray.

11.   This one is specifically for the men. You thought I forgot about you, right?

Ladies, pay attention—ladies love luxurious lingerie, and so do men.

Reciprocate for your mate and leave it on the floor.

Dating Diva—Valentine's Day—Luxe List

1. A day of beauty at Persona Day Spa—For package details visit www.personamedicalspa.com

2. Carre en Carres cashmere and silk wrap from Hermes (www.hermes.com)

3. Season tickets to the Houston Dynamo (http://web.mlsnet.com/t200/tickets/)

4. Delectable French and Italian lingerie from La Mode Lingerie (www.lamodelingerie.com)

5. Valentino one-shoulder classic, romantic red silk evening gown (www.valentino.com)

6. Ruby and diamond cuff bracelet from Valobra Fine Jewelers (www.valobra.net)

7. Hermes Rouge Red VIF 35cm Birkin Bag (www.hermes.com or Hermes Boutique 713- 623-2177)

8. Romantic St. Bart's weekend getaway via private jet (www.bomdadier.com)

9. Panthere De Cartier sapphire and diamond bracelet (www.cartier.com)

10. Jaguar XK-Series convertible from Momentum (www.momentumjaguar.net)

11. The pièce de résistance would be dinner with Carter Oosterhouse. From hanging a picture to unclogging a drain, without a doubt, this is a real man! (www.carteroosterhouse.com)

A girl can dream, right? What's on your luxe list, ladies?

What Should Men Know About Women?

While writing my book, I started writing a relationship advice column about my own personal dating adventures and the Quest for True Love. I began to share tidbits of what I was looking for in a mate. Somewhere along the way, men and women began to e-mail me directly and ask for advice about their current situations. I guess the readers related to me. How flattering! I found it fascinating, and frankly, I looked forward to checking my inbox each day as I learned that there are so many others out there with similar experiences and/or questions, just like me. The only difference was that I was willing to write about it! So let's continue the trend and start with the most common questions asked by my male readers. Yes, ladies, the *Dating Diva Adventures* have nearly a fifty-fifty demographic from all over the world, including Portugal, Sweden, Italy, Spain, London, Canada, and of course the United States! So to all of my fabulous, intelligent, charming male readers, here's what the ladies have to say in response to "What should men know about women?"

Courtney says, "No matter how educated, career-driven, and successful we alpha-females are, at the end of the day we want men to be men and we want to feel like women. We find take-charge men sexy and powerful. Now, I'm not saying we want cavemen who will beat us over the head and drag us by our ponytails, but we want men who will ask us out and then have a plan. (Do *not* play the 'I don't know, what do you want to do?' game!) Make reservations. It shows that you cared enough to plan something for our time together. Put your hand on a woman's lower back and gently guide her into a room—that gets me every time! We want to feel safe and protected. We pay attention to the little things, and they go a long way in impressing us—calling when you say you will, opening doors, standing up when we leave the table—we may be complicated beings, but we're easily impressed. Just be a man, that's all I ask! Let me feel like a woman, because many of us have to have 'balls' at work, and we do not want to wear them home."

Alva said, "Women want to be told that they are loved. Words are stronger than any possession."

Samantha said, "Women want to know how you feel; if you love us, tell us."

Susan said, "Women never get tired of hearing [the words] 'you're beautiful.'"

I say we are strong because we have to be. When we feel loved and safe we will let our guards down. We want to rest our head on your shoulder, or snuggle in your arms and allow you to be the amazing man that you are meant to be. Love us, cherish us, and we will treat you like a king.

O Canada

Dear Dating Diva:

I'm thirty-two years old. I've never been married and have no kids. I recently found myself single after four-and-a-half years of dating someone who wasn't the one. It's been about a month now, and I'm hesitant to get back in the scene, as far as dating is concerned. I've always played the dating game safe ([my] last two serious relationships have been guys I went to high school with).

Fast forward to now: About three weeks ago, a friend (and her hubby) introduced me to a guy. They raved about how attractive and nice he was but neglected to tell me he lives in Canada! So I met this guy and we hit things off, and he was amazing looking, to boot. He was going back to Canada the next day, so we exchanged Facebook information (yes, cheesy to the max). We e-mail just about every day; silly e-mails (with a flirty twist) about how our day went, what my dogs tore up, or how his hockey game went. He hasn't suggested we talk via telephone or Skype. However, we were discussing maybe putting together a Vegas trip between his friends and my friends in May or June.

Here's my dilemma—let's say we continue the daily, flirty e-mails, and we do all end up in Vegas. What should I honestly expect from the trip? Would I book a room for us or let him stay in a room with his friends and me with mine? Let's say things go well and move toward a more intimate setting? I've only spoken in person to the guy for about three hours, and if the e-mails did continue until the trip, would it be too soon for anything physical?

Does the fact that we e-mailed for a few months before the trip warrant enough "do I know this person enough to sleep with him" points? Just curious as to your thoughts?

My Dearest Olympian:

I have two simple questions for you: Do you plan on relocating to Canada? Does "O Canada" have intentions to relocate to the United

States? If the answer is no, then it's simple—no passport or work visa required! I apologize for being so blunt, but why waste your time if your roots are firmly planted in the great state of Texas?

As far as the dilemma goes, slow down! This isn't an Olympic sport. Take a breath, gorgeous! You're at a higher altitude now. I say this because women tend to over analyze everything. (This includes me!) You don't even know this man. Stop text messaging. If he's genuinely interested, let him pick up the phone and call you. He should be getting to know the real you, your sense of humor, your rate of speech, hear your amazing laugh, and what truly makes you laugh out loud. At this point, all you really know about one another is that you're both gold medalists in the alphanumeric configuration on an iPhone, right? O Canada needs to pursue you! Let him be the spirited athlete and pursue you like the champion he is!

The Meaning of True Love

From the moment we met, I knew I couldn't live without him. He was simply irresistible! His face was like no other, but to me, it felt familiar. His inner strength was mesmerizing and his personality beyond captivating. With his dirty blond hair and big eyes, I knew he was the one for me. Those closest to me suggested that I was behaving irrationally. They said he's such a baby. How could I fall for him after knowing him so briefly? With everything I have going on in my life, did I really have time for this distraction? Are you sure you're ready for a commitment? All I could think about was the sensation of pure joy I felt when in his presence. I needed him and he needed me. We were similar creatures. He enjoyed long walks, hanging out at Starbucks, and a nice run at Memorial Park on the weekends. Plus, he never laughed at me when I danced around the house like Mick Jagger in my undies. Refreshingly, he was just easy to be around. This guy was always in a good mood, seemed to love me unconditionally, and never complained when I worked too much. Confidentially, I hadn't been treating him very well.. I think I'd been a little selfish and put my own personal interests above his needs, which was ironic, as I had been down that path once before. It led me to the front door and then divorce court! I kept telling myself that this relationship was going to be different. I know that I have it in me to love another more than I love myself. I know that I have the capacity to love completely. When I arrived home one evening, his greeting was different. It was almost somber. He was shaken and visibly not himself. As I leaned toward him to give him a kiss, he threw up all over me! To my surprise, I didn't flinch in disgust. Calmly, I told him that everything was going to be alright and that Mommie was going to take care of him. For in that very moment, I realized that it took a five pound yorkie-poo—and a little vomit—to show me that I already knew the meaning of true love.

P.S. Don't worry; he threw up on a Red Sox T-shirt!

Discount Intolerant

Dear Dating Diva:

While watching a recent episode of *The Marriage Ref*, a portion of the segment was about using coupons on a date. I found the topic kind of ghetto fabulous and odd, because in my life experience, this topic has never crossed my lips. In my social circle, I've never used them before, known anyone that uses them or would use one, until tonight! Yes, you guessed it—buy one, get one free at XYZ Restaurant. I found it terribly insulting, and it really turned me off. Is this horrible? I really liked this man until the discount coupon was presented versus the black American Express! What are your thoughts on this? I mean, should this be common dating protocol not to use a coupon on a date, or am I just being a diva?

Dear Discount Intolerant:

This e-mail hits very close to home as I had the same discussion with someone close to me! However, let me put this in terms that might resonate more so. Buy one unit and get one unit free. Make sense? Would you take advantage of that fabulous offer? Yes, admit it! You would race to Dr. Livingston's office, right? Realistically, if a man were to pull out a coupon during the first month or two of dating, I'd be a little turned off. However, after three months of dating, once you're more comfortable with one another, sure, why not? It shows he's comfortable with you, knows a good deal when he finds one, and has all that extra cash to spend on those yellow roses he so thoughtfully had delivered to your home that day. My advice—focus on the big picture and aspects of dating/relationships that truly matter—communication, trust, honesty, and fidelity. Discount coupons should be the least of your worries! P.S. Jimmy Choo has a 50 percent off sale. Just mention coupon code: Dating Diva Adventures!

Chasing Harry Winston

Dear Dating Diva:

Please help me out with any advice you have. I've dated a guy for four months now. This past week, I told him I wanted to see him exclusively. He told me I had nothing to worry about and asked me to please give him time because of his new job. He told me he hopes that I'll wait for him. I said I would. This was three weeks ago and still no date or call. I still go out with others when I get a chance. What would you do? Do you think he is just going to let me go and this is the way he thinks is nice?

Dear Chasing Harry Winston:

First of all, put yourself in his Ferragamo suede loafers and imagine yourself uttering those exact words to your significant other. Get it? It's time to move on and find a man that truly wants everything that you do. Why should your life be put on hold? Now, I'm sure he's probably a super, fantastic guy but, a) he doesn't want to disappoint you, b) he doesn't want confrontation, or c) he isn't ready for a next step due to where he is in his life right now. If, in fact, he's the one for you, only time will tell. So "spring forward" and adjust that Cartier Pasha. Give him space while living your life. Note: you *can* still date him, only if he calls *you*. It's OK for a girl to keep her options open, right? Don't limit yourself, but rather, explore the world of dating and enjoy the journey. You're going to find the perfect guy. He's out there, but you need to respect your own needs as much as you do your mate's. Be kind. Be generous of heart to him but most importantly to yourself! Good luck, Chasing Harry Winston!

Net Present Value

Dear Dating Diva:

I've been seeing a guy for approximately a year now. We do not see each other as often as we would like because we are in different cities. He owns his own business so his schedule is a little bit more flexible than mine, yet I am always the one making the trip to see him. He always has an excuse as to why he cannot come see me, yet he always makes time to go out of town with his guy friends or with clients somewhere. I try to give him the benefit of the doubt, but lately my patience is wearing thin. Also, I caught him on a dating Web site recently. He is constantly online, and I confronted him about it. He said that he was just window-shopping; nothing to worry about. What are your thoughts on this? Is he telling me without telling me he is just not that into me?

Dear Net Present Value:

Repeat after me—I'm nobody's backup plan! Stop discounting yourself in this relationship. Don't you realize that you're placing his needs, wants, and desires before your own? You are condoning his behavior. You are saying that this behavior is acceptable by consistently travelling to see him. He needs to see what life is like without you and start appreciating you. Frankly, you need to stop acting like an everyday commodity. You are worth so much more. You're unique and priceless!

As for the window-shopping, put a stop and loss order on this guy ASAP! Seriously, get real! This man needs to make an effort and start coming to see you. Relationships are tough, and when one person is doing all the work, the resentment quickly becomes apparent. Long-distance relationships are expensive and exhausting, and when you're not appreciated, you are depreciating!

Chinese Food

Dear Dating Diva:

I've been dating a man for two months now. He's rather hot and cold. One minute he can't wait to be together, and in the next breath, I can barely get his attention. He says that he wants to be with me and that I make him feel like the best version of himself, but yet he pulls away from me every time we get close. What do I do? Do I acknowledge his behavior, or let it slide while this tug-of-war is tugging at my sanity? Why do men do this? Why can't they say what's on their minds without making us feel like day-old Chinese food that needs to be thrown away?

Dear Chinese Food:

Wow! Unbelievable! And as a matter of fact, one of the oldest behaviors in the dating playbook. It's the catch and release philosophy. Men want to hunt! Once they catch and dominate their prey, they move onto the next, unless you (the prey) back away or are less accessible. My point is, once they think they have you or that they have been captured, they are going to fight for their lives in order to escape your grasp. Yes, it's somewhat of a game, but nevertheless, it's human behavior. You need to decide whether you want to: a) calmly and rationally communicate with him while trying to understand how he feels, b) give him his space, and do not discuss anything with him while continually feeling like stinky leftover Chinese food, or c) find a man who is ready for all that you are without all the games. Personally, I know this story all too well. It hurts when you trust someone and give yourself to them then they pull away. Try and find your inner strength and acknowledge what you need in a relationship. Remember, open and honest communication is essential. In any relationship, whether business or professional, it's a negotiation. You will never get what you need or want unless you ask for it.

Ancient Chinese proverb says: buy a pooper-scooper, or just stop ordering the pupu platter!

Land of the Lost

Dear Dating Diva:

I've recently divorced my husband of fourteen years. I'm finding it very difficult to date as I don't know how. I went from teenager to wife to mother, and now, divorcée. I've never truly dated, so I don't know where to go to meet new people. Where do I start? Where do I go? Any advice is appreciated.

Dear Land of the Lost:

You are not alone! I recently met two "Land of the Lost" inductees that are in the same boat. I must introduce you!

Step 1: Get out there! Accept as many social invitations as humanly possible, without neglecting the kiddos! Try this: happy hour, cocktail parties, restaurant openings, obtain a gym membership, donate spare time to a charity, learn to play golf, join a tennis team, take a "sushi singles" cooking class, or attend a church singles group.

Step 2: Change your routine! Get out and meet new people. Stop going through the drive-thru and start socializing! Go grab dinner by yourself at a fabulous restaurant. You'd be surprised how many times you'll get approached!

Step 3: Get out of your comfort zone! Leave yourself open to the possibility of meeting someone new. Solo activities, whether going to a movie, a batting cage, dining, or reading a book outside at Starbucks, will only encourage random encounters with others.

Step 4: Don't always travel in packs! This deters men from approaching and making contact.

Hint: If you are at a cocktail party, make sure you create an open area around yourself that creates an approachable environment for the right target audience. No crossed arms, no negative or closed-off body language, no girlie group huddles, and most importantly, implement Step #5.

Step 5: Smile! Happy people attract other happy people. A simple smile makes you more approachable to others! So "purrfect" your inner Cheshire cat and stock up on that whitening toothpaste!

By following these initial steps, you'll ultimately guide yourself out of the land of the lost!

Reader Comment from Facebook:

Once again, excellent advice! I especially like #4. Even [we] confident men have a hard time approaching women who are surrounded by other women. I always get the sense that women who are with their friends don't really want a guy coming up and hitting on them. So I would never approach them. However, going solo does make the experience a little more daunting for the woman who is seeking a relationship, because many men are jerks and a woman's friends provide a protective barrier (of sorts) against the overly aggressive man. Going without that protection can be a little intimidating to some people. But still, you get no rewards in life without risk.

Good Dates Gone Bad

Through my various life experiences, I've discovered that the one constant in basic everyday life skills is a good positive attitude. Every day when I wake up, I make a cognizant decision to be happy. I choose to not let the drama created by others into my world and keep those closest to me protected by the drama that sometimes is inevitable. In dating, I believe that we must not only accept a date in the good-spirited nature in which the invitation was extended but also to make it fun, light-hearted and enjoyable. So when people tell me that they had a bad date, I must ask why?

Here are a few reader snippets of good dates gone bad. Enter at your own risk and with a sense of humor, people!

Date 1:

I'm on a date with a girl and she happens to see her ex-boyfriend in the restaurant. As she excuses herself from the table to freshen up, I see her exiting stage left with the ex-boyfriend. What do I do now? Do I call her out on this crappy behavior? What do you think?

(*Names and expletives removed to protect the innocent.)

Diva Response:

Seriously, like you have to ask? Consider yourself lucky. This girl obviously has no manners or self-respect. If what you're saying is 100 percent accurate, this selfish girl isn't worth the time of day, and frankly it sounds like the guy she left with is a better match. I mean really, he snaked another guy's date and didn't even pick up the check. Disgusting! You, on the other hand, appear to care about people, including yourself, and didn't cause a scene by chasing after her. Kudos to you. Move on, let it go, and find a *woman*!

Real women do not behave like this. Trust me!

Date 2:

A very close guy friend set me up on a date with a man who was recently divorced. He's a great guy, but I think he drinks way too much to overcompensate for the divorce. After our first date, I ended up having to drive him to his sister's house and drop him off and then take a cab home. He's called me to apologize, but I cannot seem to get over the fact that he's just not in a place to date. Hence, the overdrinking. If you were me, what would you do?

Diva Response:

Oh my God! I think I know this guy! No joke. If he drives a red ... well, never mind. I digress.

You have a forgiving nature and I admire that. However, his issues are not yours. He is most likely a good person, but he was responsible for you and your safety. A man needs to behave like a man, and a lady needs to be a class act at all times! Bravo for doing the right thing by driving him home, but he needs to deal with his issues, and you need to find someone as generous of heart as you are. Be his friend, accept his apology, and in time, who knows what'll happen!

Date 3:

I'm a twenty-two-year-old female and have been dating a fairly successful real estate developer for the last two months. He's super cute, fun, and great in bed. I really like this guy, but something happened the other night, and I am really uncomfortable even talking to him about it. Basically, we went to a Mexican restaurant for dinner. We ordered margaritas—one after the other. I was having so much fun, until the check came. Like always, he took care of the bill. Unfortunately, when the waiter returned, his credit card was declined. I didn't know what to do. I mean, I'm a student and don't make a lot of money, but I offered to pay for the bill. I can barely afford my rent; let alone picking up a hundred dollar-plus dinner. Should I ask him to reimburse me for the dinner? I think he should at least offer, but then am I a bad person for accepting his money?

Diva Response:

OK, this is a hot topic for sure! I am so sorry that you had to experience this. I empathize with your situation and would suggest that you let this one go. I know this seems like unusual advice, but he is most likely as embarrassed, if not more so, than you are. If he's worth it, he'll give you the money when he's able. In this economy, times are tough for everyone, so why make a situation even more uncomfortable than it already is? The one thing I do know is that he'll be more prepared on his next date with you, and he'll bring cash!

Guys and Dolls, dating is a full contact sport! You're going to get dirty! Dating (and relationships) requires consistency, communication, the commitment to understanding yourself, your limitations, and most importantly, heart! Not all dating issues are deal-breakers, and not all dates are perfect. Learn to communicate your needs and desires, and as always, respect yourself when dating. Do not let anyone treat you poorly, and do not treat your date poorly.

Thirty-four

I made a list
I checked it twice
Did I prefer naughty
Or did I need nice?

After first dates with thirty-three
Could thirty-four set me free?

I asked
I prayed
Yet you found me
But I could not see what was in front of me

For you are a gift from up above
Who warms my heart and brings me love

I hope that I can only be
As wonderful as you are to me

Eternity

I feel at peace
My soul does rest
Although my body does protest
You spark something inside of me
That heightens every fantasy
I think of you
I come alive.
With bated breath there's no compromise
For you are someone that I can see
Spending all eternity

For those who embrace the Quest for True love and savor each breathtaking moment along the way.

Text Obsessed

Dear Dating Diva:

I started hanging out with this girl two months ago and now we're pretty much together all the time. My concern is that she keeps texting on her Blackberry. If we're watching a movie, she's still looking at her Blackberry, answering texts/calls from friends. I talked to her about it, and she just says, "It's a friend." I know it's not work. She's a waitress/college student. I just wonder why she can't focus on us and our time together. Right now, I just feel like being a jerk about it all and telling her to screw off, because deep down I feel like there's someone else in the picture. What do you think?

Dear Text Obsessed:

Here's the deal—when a woman is spending time with the man of her dreams, she's totally focused on that man. She doesn't pick up her Blackberry and text her friends. My advice—talk with her and tell her that it's highly inconsiderate to be texting when you're together. As far as who she's texting, who the heck cares! This is about you and no one else. If she keeps up the obsessive texting, kick her to the curb. She's not worth the effort and frankly doesn't value you or your relationship. You deserve better. Keep in mind that one of the critical success factors in any relationship, whether business or personal, is respect. If you don't respect yourself, no one else will, either!

Rock and a Hard Place

Dear Dating Diva:

I've been dating a girl exclusively for the last two months and things have been going great. The other night, she told me that she loved me. I didn't know what to say, so I said I care about her very much. The problem is, now things are weird. When we go out, she barely holds my hand, she doesn't want to sleep over, and she seems really pissed off all the time. She won't admit it, but I know that she's mad that I didn't say "I love you" back, but now I feel pressured to say something that I'm not sure I actually mean. What do I do?

Dear Rock and a Hard Place:

As the old saying goes, say what you mean and mean what you say. Here's the issue:

1) She said that she loved you and you didn't return the sentiment. Now, she's vulnerable and this makes her angry. 2) You feel obligated to return the sentiment, although you don't mean it, as you believe that this might make things go back to normal.

End Result: You say something that you don't mean, resent her for it in the long run, and later break up with her because of it.

My advice: Have a talk with her and tell her what you do like about her. Try to humanize yourself and the relationship all while making her feel special. Saying that you love someone versus showing them can sometimes be two totally different things. Sometimes it's the personal, heartfelt sentiments, versus the words "I love you" that resonate and make us feel more special.

Compromise without Commitment

Dear Dating Diva:

I've been dating a man for the last ten months and I really like him. The problem is that I travel about three days a week for work. This makes dating really challenging, as my schedule is unpredictable! He wants me to stop travelling as much, but it's how I make a living. Plus, I enjoy my job. I want to spend more time with him, but why should I have to compromise my work and income for a new relationship without a commitment?

It just seems like I'm being asked to sacrifice, and I don't think it's fair. What do you think?

Dear Compromise without Commitment:

Without knowing the complete dynamics of the relationship, I would tend to agree with you. If he cares for you, he must know by now that you enjoy your job. Also, he must realize that having a job in today's tough economic climate is rare! If I were you, I would explain this to him along with what your work and personal goals are. Yes, you can talk about where the relationship is headed. Now's the time! Try and find out why he's pushing you. Jealousy? Loneliness? Ugh, no, pass! If his request involves true, loving companionship and he's genuinely trying to build something long term with you, then you're going to have to come up with some sort of compromise. Relationships are work and do require sacrifice. They also require a commitment. You can have it all. However, you're going to have to figure out how to create a balance between work and your relationship. Find a balance that works best for you, your job, your man, and ultimately get that commitment with a little compromise!

Trapped

Dear Dating Diva:

My girlfriend and I have been together for about a year. Lately she's been talking a lot about getting engaged, marriage, and kids. I'm just not ready yet. She knows that my job hasn't been going that great. That's one of the reasons we moved in together three months ago. I love her and want to be with her, but I'm just not ready for marriage. Over the last couple of weeks, I've noticed that her sexual appetite has been unusually extreme. It's just not like her, so I did what any normal guy would do; I looked at her birth control pills. If I'm looking at it right, it appears that she is missing several days at a time. I am feeling a sense of betrayal right now and almost like she's trying to trap me into marriage with a pregnancy. What do I do?

Dear Trapped:

This isn't an easy one to answer, as you have a lot of moving parts in your relationship. I guess the first thing I'd like to address is trust. Without trust, you have no relationship. Now, let's discuss contraception. Contraception is just as much a man's responsibility. It takes two! Really? Shocking, I know! If you believe that she isn't taking the pill, then you need to be responsible and use a condom. Wrap it up! Either way, it sounds like you two have a lot to talk about. Truly, I'm not a relationship expert, so please go talk to someone who loves you both and can provide sound, rational advice with the best of intentions. If you truly love your girlfriend, talk to her and work through this. Obviously, you have some concerns that need to be addressed ASAP. Do it head on and you can never go wrong. Good luck to you both.

To Know Me

If you want to know me, you must take time to listen, understand, empathize, show compassion, communicate, and build trust.

If you want to know me, you must reveal your true self. You must share your desires, fears, dreams, laughter, and accomplishments.

If you want to know me, you must allow me to be strong and at times be weak while building me up when I'm down.

If you want to know me, you must hold my hand, look into my eyes, see my soul, and feel my love at the very tips of your toes.

If after all of this, you still don't know me, you might consider getting to know yourself.

For in order to truly love, you must love yourself, respect yourself, and realize that true love is more than the physical and can take on a much greater meaning that far outweighs this humble existence.

Creeped Out

Dear Dating Diva:

I'm in college and my mom is "friending" my guy friends on Facebook. Now they are commenting on her photos and it's freaking me out. My mom is young and she's pretty, but I don't think it's right that my friends are her friends on Facebook. I think she's crossed the line and should be acting like a grown-up. Don'tcha think? I mean really, it's not like I want my guy friends hitting on my mom and then talking about it at school. I'm totally creeped out here. Help!

Dear Creeped Out:

Let's cut to the chase. "De-friend" your mom and explain the situation to her. Consider "de-friending" the schmucks that comment on her photos too. It sounds like they aren't your friends, because they obviously don't respect you. Frankly, your mom sounds a little like she's longing for some attention, but it shouldn't come at the cost of damaging your relationship with her. Explain to your mom that these are your friends and that this is your venue to communicate with them and you hope she understands. Best case scenario, she understands and respects your candor. Worst case scenario, you'll have to shut down your Facebook page and let it hibernate for a while.

One Hundred Things

Dear Dating Diva:

I'm writing you because I'm not sure where else to turn as I don't know anyone [who] won't think I'm crazy. I've been dating a guy for four months and I'm not sure how I feel about him or if I really know him at all. How do I know for sure? Any advice would really ease my mind right now. What to do?

Dating Diva Response:

Believe it or not, I know how you feel! Like you, I've been in a similar circumstance. Personally, I need to challenge myself in order to see what I know about someone and how I validate it versus going solely on my emotions. Yes, I'm an analytical freak. I'm female, hello!

So here's what I'd recommend—make a list of one hundred things that you know about the person. You have two hours to accomplish this task. If within that timeframe you can list tangible points of interest, you might actually know this person and something about his character. Here's an example of how simple and yet truly romantic this exercise can be.

One Hundred Things

1. His mom and dad have been married for over forty years

2. He has one sister and two brothers

3. He was born in London

4. His family visited him this summer

5. He graduated college and has his MBA

6. He is head coach of a soccer team and was previously assistant coach for two years

7. He moved to the US by himself

8.   His favorite meal—his mom's lamb with mint jelly

9.   His favorite dessert—anything chocolate

10. His favorite color—blue

11. His normal Starbucks order: double shot espresso

12. He likes to pheasant hunt

13. He was chubby as a child

14. He loves his two dogs

15. He adopted one dog from pound. It had been malnourished

16. His life is coaching his kids, students, dogs and soccer

17. He misses his family and friends in London

18. He feels most alone when he's grocery shopping

19. He likes to drink breakfast tea—milk, no sugar

20. He has a massive appetite

21. He's caring, compassionate, loyal, respected, stellar coach, and kids love him

22. He wants to get married and have children

23. He's a blinker

24. His beer of choice: Guinness

25. He likes to mimic boxing moves and look at his reflection when he pumps gas

26. He's fabulously romantic

27. He loves art and nature

28. He's an avid boxer

29. He has a tattoo that represents his gym's boxing team on his back

30. He's incredibly smart and articulate

31. He's passionate

32. He's loving and nurturing

33. He's charitable and volunteers regularly

34. He has blue eyes, fantastic lips, perfect teeth, and a wicked smile

35. He has a third nipple. Think Chandler Bing!

36. He's beautiful inside and out

37. He's a great cuddler

38. He smells amazing

39. His version of a manicure equates to biting his nails

40. He has very long fingernail beds

41. He has pretty hands

42. He is considerate and mannerly

43. His greatest fear—never to have kids

44. He loves green tea with sushi

45. His last car was a Jeep Cherokee

46. He has been handcuffed before

47. He believes in taking one's own life, if life is not deemed worth living

48. He despises those who are cruel to animals

49. He's an excellent kisser and amazingly intimate

50. He's sincere

51. He's attentive

52. He has strong core values

53. He has a temper—when it comes to sports standards, accountability for one's actions

54. He plans to spend Thanksgiving with his family

55. He hopes to spend Christmas in London or Costa Rica

56. His date of birth—2-11

57. He loves Prodigy, Francis and the Machine, U2, Coldplay, oldies and Alan Jackson

58. He knows how to hold hands properly

59. He's very affectionate

60. He loves the ocean and coastline

61. He started his own soccer team

62. He coaches sixteen year old students and at the local university

63. He's a positive person

64. He's a good driver when he's not trying to kiss me (that doesn't mean stop, though)

65. He's motivating

66. He's quick-witted

67. He's right-handed and right-footed

68. He's second and third toes are almost equal in length

69. He's very ticklish

70. He has a mole on center of his back and several on his scalp

71. He has his own sense of style.

72. He's thoughtful

73. His eyes speak volumes

74. He loves bananas and strawberries

75. He watches his weight

76. He enjoys bagels with fat free cream cheese

77. He loves motocross

78. He's remodeling his house

79. He has peed in a shower before

80. He doesn't stand in front of the mirror naked

81. His favorite movie—*Layer Cake*

82. His ring tone: "Omen"—Prodigy song

83. His favorite books: soccer—Beckham and people he thinks are most like him or who he strives to be

84. His mother loves her flower garden

85. His cologne: Hugo Boss and Jean Paul Gauthier

86. He loves Indian food (curry!) and Persian food

87. He loves games

88. He's rather selfless

89. He doesn't care for his nose

90. His nose has been broken

91. His nose was reset by owner of the gym—twice

92. His left shoulder is bothersome

93. When he's stressed, he runs his hands through his hair

94. When he's tired, he says he's "shattered"

95. When he likes something, it's "super fantastic"

96. He's not computer literate

97. He's devoted to his passion—soccer

98. He would prefer to live in the country

99. His favorite colors—purple and gold, baby!

100. He's humble

Take my method for getting to know someone in the good-spirited nature that it's meant. No cheating—you must do this from pure memory! As far as how you feel, always trust the tingle in your toes and the magical feeling you get when he enters a room. For that cannot be created in any laboratory. Chemistry is critical! Dig deep and challenge yourself. Then see what this man knows about you. Do you have a good foundation to build from? Only "one hundred things" will tell!

READER COMMENT FROM FACEBOOK:

I couldn't agree with you more. My family members always tell me to write out a list. Once you do that, it's like the energy starts to attract you with that exact person you described. You truly have a gift! Lots of us girls have such mixed emotions about our men these days!

Average Girl

Dear Dating Diva:

It seems like you have an amazing and glamorous life with all your stories. Most girls would kill to be like you, if only for a day. So for all us average girls like me, we want to know what's the difference in looking like you, getting asked out all the time, and going on all these adventures?

Dear Average Girl:

Please know that I appreciate the flattery to some extent, but like you, I consider myself an average girl. Being pretty is a luxury and one not to be taken lightly. It does not allow for arrogance, a sense of entitlement, or poor behavior. I do not define myself by the way that I look, but rather, I consistently seek to improve myself through my words, actions, beliefs, and encounters with others. Although I do enjoy a day at Arena Day Spa now and again!

So to answer your question, I guess the difference would be that I've chosen not to shy away from chance encounters. (Thank you, Peet's Coffee at Hobby Airport.) For example, I vacation, dine, and go to movies by myself on occasion. Frankly, it's liberating. Try it! You never know who you'll meet on the adventure ahead. Some would attest that I'm very independent. Certainly I consider myself more open than most to the opportunity of meeting someone new, but now the question is, are you?

So here's my challenge, Average Girl, are you ready? I want you to go and put yourself out there. Live a little! I want you to do something out of character and then write me back telling me about your adventure. Trust me; if I can do it, you can too! I look forward to your return. Now, let the Adventures of Average Girl begin. No cape or superhero mask required.

Buenos Aires

I began my adventures nearly twenty years ago when I became a flight attendant for Eastern Airlines. At that time, it was what I referred to as my conduit to the world and what I now refer to as "adventure travel." It was an opportunity to make a little money, gain some real-life work experience, and live out my dreams. Who could refuse, right?

So after accepting the job, I purchased the book *Let's Go,* in order to plot my travel wish list. First on the list—Buenos Aires, Argentina! After five months of employment and the added skill of making a screwdriver under my belt, I was able to save up enough money to afford not-so-diva-like accommodations. Nevertheless, I was determined and Buenos Aires-bound.

It was a grueling flight, but once we landed, any aches and pains I had experienced from the cramped, non-reclining coach seat next to the lavatory suddenly escaped me. With my luggage in tow, I headed toward the designated taxi stand area. I was incredibly nervous not knowing the language, but I was quick with my prewritten flash cards! Yes, I packed good, old fashioned flash cards which named the desired location in which I'd rest my head for the evening. As I handed the driver my destination card, he smiled and quickly chuckled. Without pause, he turned to look at me and began speaking in broken English. At that moment, he seemed thrilled just to be practicing his English. After a good twenty-minute ride, he dropped me off at my hotel. After checking in, I realized that one of my bags hadn't made it into the hotel. I was irritated at myself for being so careless and devastated thinking that pretty much every article of my clothing would be lost. Within minutes, the driver reappeared with my bag in hand. I couldn't believe my good fortune. I thanked him profusely, grabbed my bag, and began to walk toward my room. The room was cozy and clean. Its only window looked upon a painted mural of children in a playground and a beautiful courtyard covered by lush trees. Although I couldn't see anyone, I could hear laughter from below, which provided a sense of comfort and peace. I was off to a good start, but I needed rest from my flight before continuing my adventure.

The next day I woke up, grabbed a quick coffee, and raced out the door. Not knowing where I was going, I just decided to let my internal compass be my guide and explore my immediate surroundings. My goal when travelling is to see and experience as much of the culture from a local's perspective as I can. Like others, I do enjoy the touristy-type attractions, but the thrill of just exploring makes my heart race and makes me feel alive. I walked aimlessly for hours and stumbled across what was once possibly a bridge or dock of some sort. It was partially washed away, but what remained was breathtaking. I began to walk across the bridge toward the water. At the end of the bridge, there were two stone lions sitting guard. Exhausted from my walk, I decided to sit down and let the moment consume me. I remember telling myself to mentally capture photos so that I would never forget what I could only refer to as visual perfection. To this day, I vividly recall the warm sun and gentle caress of the breeze as it brushed across my face and the cool spray mist of the waves onto my skin. For this memory would later become my safe and peaceful escape. A single moment captured in time. As I sat in silence with only my thoughts and a magnificent view to keep me company, a man walked up behind me. At first I was startled, but as my eyes adjusted from the light, his presence calmed me. His name was Guillermo, and in the blink of an eye, my adventures and that of a Dating Diva were inspired. As you might suspect, we had two magical and romantic weeks together. Other than Paris, it was probably one of the most romantic periods of my life.

So in the end, my lessons learned while sharing my life, loves, opinions, and adventures with you are that I am forever a romantic adventure-seeker at heart. However, unlike the lion statues, I cannot be tamed, nor will my zest for life.

For those individuals who have tried to tame me, I applaud you for your efforts. Thank you for loving me.

For those who have wished to silence me, know that my words are just as important as yours. The only difference is that I am unashamed or apologetic for the life that I lead and the choices that I make. What you've failed to recognize is that I am became stronger because of you. Thank you.

For I am concrete in who I am and who I am evolving into with each passing day. For in the end, my journey led me home.

I discovered that true love was inside me all along and in every new friend who so openly shared their lives with me. For you accepted and encouraged my journey and that has left me forever grateful, humbled, and filled with love. Now the only outstanding question is, will he?

About the Author

When she was 18 years old, Lori Lemon-Geshay moved from Georgia to New York City to become a Flight Attendant for Eastern Airlines. With her girl next door looks and southern charm, she was quickly discovered by a well-known modeling agency. Lori was able to land such notable campaigns for Coty Cosmetics, LA Gear, Country Time Lemonade and Pepsi. She later branched out into acting and appeared briefly on *Another World*, and *The Days and Nights of Molly Dodd*. Amongst her numerous professional accomplishments, Lori is a highly ranked IT sales professional, specializing in Oracle and Hyperion. Presently, she enjoys writing her relationship advice column, and designing custom diamond jewelry. Lori is a constant in the Houston social scene and boasts a fan club of Houston's elite.

Content and Graphics

The graphic artwork attached to this document have been created expressly by and for Lori Lemon-Geshay. The unlimited rights to use this artwork have been paid for. The illustrator (and his/her agent, Caricature Connection), only reserve the right to use the image for promotional purposes.

www.ingramcontent.com/pod-product-compliance
Lightning Source LLC
LaVergne TN
LVHW042137040326
832903LV00011B/283/J